Good Governance for Nonprofits

Developing Principles and Policies for an Effective Board

Fredric L. Laughlin

Robert C. Andringa

American Management Association

New York • Brussels • Chicago • Mexico City • San Francisco
Shanghai • Tokyo • Washington, D.C.

This publication is designed to provide accurate and authoritative information in regard to the subject matter covered. It is sold with the understanding that the publisher is not engaged in rendering legal, accounting, or other professional service. If legal advice or other expert assistance is required, the services of a competent professional person should be sought.

Library of Congress Cataloging-in-Publication Data

Laughlin, Fredric L.
    Good governance for nonprofits : developing principles and policies for an effective board / Fredric L. Laughlin and Robert C. Andringa.
        p.   cm.
    Includes bibliographical references and index.
    ISBN-13: 978-0-8144-1594-8
    ISBN-10: 0-8144-1594-6
    1. Nonprofit organizations—Management.   2. Boards of directors.
3. Corporate governance.   I. Andringa, Robert C.   II. Title.
    HD62.6.L38 2007
    658.4'22—dc22   2007018430

Printing number

10 9 8 7 6 5 4 3 2 1

Contents

MS Word files of the materials in Appendix B are available at
www.amacombooks.org/go/goodgovnonprofits.

Foreword

Without a meaningful mission, an organization has no purpose.
Without effective implementation of that mission, an organization fails.
Good governance is essential for both a meaningful mission
and its effective implementation.

While much of my experience with governance has occurred serving as a CEO and on the Boards of Directors of public for-profit
corporations, I have also had the opportunity to serve on the
Boards of both large and small nonprofits. Although the share-
holders and their expectations for results are more clearly defined
for the for-profit organization, the accountability and ownership
of results for both the for-profit and nonprofit ultimately rests with
the Board of Directors. The effective implementation of this responsibility is not determined only by a monetary measurement
but also includes whether there has been a change and improvement in the lives of the people working for and being served by the
organization.

The widely publicized failures and bad governance practices of
some organizations have caught the attention of Congress, other
regulating bodies, and the general public. For the for-profit public

corporation, this has resulted in specific legislation adding new standards of compliance, procedures, and disclosures with corresponding penalties for failure to comply. Some of these new standards will no doubt be extended to nonprofits. Their ultimate objective is to set a higher standard of accountability for the leadership and the governing boards of organizations that have been granted the right and the privilege of contributing to the welfare of our society. Governing boards should, and in an increasing way will, be asked to demonstrate, i.e., measure and disclose, whether the organization is being effective in fulfilling its mission and whether the board is effective in its oversight responsibility.

These new standards and expectations of performance will require boards to be aware of best practices, have a better understanding of their role in reviewing, approving, evaluating and, where needed, supporting the actions and decisions of the CEO. They must also continue to know and follow how the people charged with doing the work of the organization are growing and being developed—not only what they are doing but who they are becoming.

Board education and training for nonprofits will become increasingly important. The Roadmap that Fred Laughlin and Bob Andringa describe in this book will be very helpful to nonprofit boards, particularly in the way they walk you through the development of the Board Policies Manual (or BPM). The BPM is really a governance management system that helps boards and senior management understand their respective roles and functions and become more effective in their performance and their accountability.

A BPM can be developed without an extraordinary tax on resources and once integrated into the governance of an organization it can serve as the core document for organizing all future board policies. It will be "a best friend" and guide to the board in general and to the Chair and the CEO in particular. If you are on a nonprofit Board, I encourage you to use the Roadmap suggested by Bob and Fred. Your board work will become more effective, efficient, and rewarding.

The future will require more commitment, competency, and time on behalf of board members. You must always be willing to learn and to serve. You must be ready to raise the tough questions with a willingness to compromise on the non-essentials. And once the decision is made, you must give your full support to the CEO and the task of management to implement the board's policies and decisions. This book will help you fulfill that critical role in your organization.

C. William Pollard
Chairman Emeritus,
ServiceMaster Corp.

Preface

This book is written for CEOs and board members who seek to improve the way they govern their nonprofit organizations. We have written it in the form of a "roadmap" to guide leaders along what we have found to be the most direct route to excellence in all aspects of the governance function. We believe that the principles and practices that are embodied in this roadmap apply to nonprofits of every size, type, degree of complexity, and present level of governance efficiency and effectiveness.

Over the past 15 years scandals in both the for-profit and not-for-profit sectors of the economy have jerked awake the hitherto sleepy function of governance. Suddenly boards of directors are expected to carry out their responsibilities with skill, resolve, knowledge, strength, and sensitivity. Public pressure has prompted Congress and state governments to pass laws, form oversight bodies, and issue reams of regulations that are intended to govern the governors of organizations. The wave of rules has spawned a new growth of consultants, authors, and advisors, who, in their attempt to help, sometimes add to the pressure for an organization to "do something"!

In the nonprofit sector, our experience is that most CEOs and boards of directors have sought a balanced response to the increased attention to governance. While they admit that their structures and processes could use some sprucing up, they don't believe that they need to overhaul their whole system—a renovation perhaps, but not a razing and rebuild. Even so, there is still the question of where and how do nonprofit organizations adjust their governance models to find that balanced response? This book is designed to help nonprofit organizations answer that question. It grew out of our work with CEOs and boards as they sought to improve their governance structures and processes. We developed an approach that has been both effective and economical in terms of time and money. We have called this approach a roadmap as it is easy to follow and it contains distinguishable steps and milestones along the way.

At the heart of the approach is a document that we call the Board Policies Manual (BPM), which contains a clear articulation of the strategic direction of the organization, the way the board is to be structured, how it will govern the organization, and what specific direction it has for the CEO. The roadmap to good governance, therefore, is simply the path that we recommend for a nonprofit board to develop its BPM and employ it to implement the practices and principles that characterize an efficient and effective governance model.

We discuss the roadmap in three distinct phases or legs of the journey, which are:

1. **Committing to the concept.** Developing a BPM will require full buy-in from the board and the CEO. If it's done right, the exercise of developing the BPM will touch every key principle of governance and the board will need to be involved with every step.

2. **Developing the BPM**—Notwithstanding the importance of the BPM for a board, its development does not have to be a daunting task. We have worked with a time-tested way to develop a BPM, which has been employed successfully by nonprofits of various size, type, and complexity. The method, of course, assumes the earlier commitment as it will tap the board's expertise and rely on its follow-through.

3. **Integrating the BPM**—The BPM is not intended to be a static document that addresses a single need at a specific point in time. Its role is to be an integral part of the governance process on a continuing basis. To ensure that it reflects the board's current thinking, the BPM must be kept up-to-date and relevant.

The consistent product of this basic three-step process is an efficient, effective, and durable model of governance. This sequence of steps is admittedly commonplace and probably draws only a twitch of the needle on the excitement meter. Yet, we have found that (1) **each step** in the process **is necessary** and (2) the **overall process is sufficient** to move an organization from its present level of governance to where it wants to go.

Most of the space in the book is given to the actual development of the BPM where we guide you through each step in the process. We give you a template to follow along with some specific policy language that you may want to use. We also suggest options for the policies in the various sections.

We believe that by following the roadmap the reader will encounter all of the basic principles that characterize good models of governance. We designed the roadmap to be used without an interpreter or a consultant. Accordingly, we cover each "leg of the trip" as if the reader needs the explanation and rationale for including it. Some readers will observe that their organizations have already completed that leg, i.e., incorporated the particular principles or adopted the practices, and therefore will be able to skip to the next leg of the journey. We trust that, regardless of how near or far the organization's governance model is to the target destination, its leaders will find the roadmap useful for outlining the remainder of the route.

Our approach to good governance owes a great deal to the work of John Carver, whose writings have contributed so much to the field of governance for nonprofit organizations. This book also reflects our backgrounds, Fred's from his 29 years at Price Waterhouse working with for-profit organizations and Bob's from his 25 years with not-for-profit organizations. We often see boards with members from these different backgrounds who have what appear to be conflicting views of how a nonprofit organization ought to be run. Those from the for-profit sector may see the nonprofit organization as requiring more discipline and "sound business practices," a message that may come across to others as insensitive or incompatible with the culture of the organization, e.g., a charity, museum, housing authority, trade association, education institution, or inner-city ministry. We do not see this as an either/or decision. On the contrary, boards that respect both points of view usually preserve the culture of the organization on one hand while exercising good stewardship of resources on the other. Our approach to moving the organization along the continuum toward excellence has that balance in mind and we have found boards who have honored both points of view benefit from leveraging the differences in perspectives rather than being split by them.

Finally, while we are confident that the approach outlined in this book incorporates all the theoretical and academic underpinnings of excellence in governance, we want it to be practical. We want it to be employed in bringing about improvements in the way boards and CEOs lead their organizations. To that end, we have included within the book a BPM template (Appendix A) and a list of material that we have posted to the AMA website. To borrow from a popular commercial slogan, the theme of this book with respect to making significant improvements to your governance is "You can do it. We can help."

Acknowledgments

This book started out as a short monograph for our clients. Then we talked to Adrienne Hickey, Editor-in-Chief of AMACOM Books, who looked at our booklet on why nonprofits need a Board Policies Manual (BPM) and told us that it ought to be a book that actually explained how to develop a BPM. She was right. What was originally a pamphlet selling the BPM concept became a book on how to make it happen. Throughout the writing and editing process, Adrienne has been a steady cheerleader and a pleasure to work with. AMACOM has many talented people behind their excellent publications and we now are indebted to several of them, including Jim Bessent, who patiently led us from a rough manuscript to a completed book. Also, Alice Manning applied her thoughtful copyediting skills to lift the fog on many a page and paragraph.

As two guys who have for some time worked in the area of nonprofit governance, perhaps a rare but growing breed, we acknowledge those on whose work we have tried to build. Both of us enjoy sound theory that works in practice, so we have enormous respect for Dr. John Carver, whose seminal works in nonprofit governance have given shape and substance to the subject over the past fifteen years. In addition, BoardSource and its indispensable resources have allowed us and the organizations with whom we work to be stimulated by best practices. We learn constantly through their good work.

Our clients, however, have taught us the most. We like to gather principles, techniques, and practices that work over and over and these organizations and their leaders have provided the laboratory for learning that gives us confidence in the recommendations that we offer in this book. Prime examples are the four organizations [Miriam's Kitchen, the Translational Genomics Research Institute, the Association of Graduates at West Point, and World Vision, Inc.], whose stories are highlighted in Chapter 12. Between us we have interacted with thousands of board members and hundreds of CEOs. Their positive response to what we are now putting into this book makes our work meaningful.

Leaders in the corporate world like Bill Pollard, who graciously wrote our Foreword, have always inspired us. These busy men and women have invested their considerable skills in serving on boards of nonprofits, helping to bring order out of sometimes chaos in this important social sector of our economy.

Other consultants and friends have encouraged us in our work with boards. Dale Lefever, John Pearson, Rob Stevenson, Scott McBride, John Knubel, Bill Crothers, Ted Engstrom, Nancy Axelrod, Susan Whealler Johnston and many more provided insights and suggestions along the way.

Finally, because time with our families and grandchildren was so often sacrificed to meet approaching deadlines, we would acknowledge the support and love that we have received from each member, but especially from our wives Maralee Laughlin and Sue Andringa. These special women need no book, or policy manual for that matter, on good governance of the most important organization in our society—the family.

Fred Laughlin and Bob Andringa

CHAPTER I

Got Good Governance?

All nonprofit boards have one thing in common. They do not work.
—Peter Drucker

Since you are looking at a book entitled *Good Governance for Nonprofits,* chances are that you are a board member, a CEO, or a staff member of a nonprofit organization. If so, you are in good company. There are almost two million nonprofit organizations in the United States, all of which have boards and most of which have someone functioning as the CEO. Tens of thousands of these nonprofits have sizable staffs.

While you may not agree totally with Peter Drucker's rather stark assessment of nonprofit boards, we suspect that you can think of areas where your board could be more efficient and effective. Here again, you would not be alone. There is no perfect board. Members and officers of nonprofit boards, assisted by authors and consultants, are training critical eyes on the structures and processes of their boards and coming away with lists of areas for improvement—in some cases rather long lists. The problem, therefore, given the usually limited human and financial resources of nonprofits, has become less a matter of what needs to be done and more a question of how one attacks this to-do list in a systematic way.

Four Organizations That Have Done It

Here are four nonprofit organizations whose boards were confronted with a list of improvements in their governance model. In Chapter 12, we have documented the course of action that each of them took to address its list. For now, we will simply introduce the four organizations and their situations.

> *Miriam's Kitchen* has served homeless men and women in Washington, DC, for almost 25 years. Over the years, it has survived on an ounce of cash and a ton of heart. After the turn of the century, however, it stabilized its management and its operations and found itself moving from a somewhat unsettled adolescent organization to a more secure adult. Its board was still populated by highly committed and dedicated directors, but it needed a governance structure that would better serve this now mature organization.
>
> *The Translational Genomics Research Institute (TGen)* was a high-risk gamble by an unusual blend of public and private entities in Arizona, which together put down $120 million to bring the biotech industry to the state. TGen was the "anchor store" in what was expected to be one of the top biotech malls in the world. The board that was formed to govern TGen included some of the most powerful people in the state, starting with the governor. From the beginning of this impressive organization, its board needed a structure and a set of related processes that would accommodate the diversity of its members and the gravitas of so many heavy hitters.
>
> *The Association of Graduates* (AOG) serves the United States Military Academy at West Point and its unique column of graduates known as the Long Gray Line. Although West Point

was established by President Jefferson in 1802, the AOG was not formed until 1869. Its original purpose was to help bring together graduates who had fought on opposing sides in the Civil War. As the academy approached its bicentennial in 2002, therefore, the AOG was an old association—and its governance structure showed it. In 2004, the chair of the AOG board assembled a task force to identify ways for it to bring its governance into the twenty-first century.

World Vision International is one of the largest and best-known charitable organizations in the world. For over 50 years, World Vision has faithfully served poor and hungry people around the globe with an efficiency and effectiveness that few organizations can match. In 1998, World Vision, Inc., the U.S. partner of World Vision International, hired a CEO who had little experience with nonprofits, but who knew the value of good governance; with the support of his board chairman, he sought help in upgrading the board's structure and processes.

These organizations have very different missions that affect the lives of very different constituencies. They are unlike in size, age, complexity, and geographical reach. The profile of their boards is also different, as are their bylaws. Yet for all of their dissimilarities, these organizations share the common experience of following a course of action that has led to marked improvement in the way their boards govern their organizations. We call that course of action a *roadmap*, and in this book we describe what it is, why it so effective, and how any nonprofit board can take advantage of it.

Who Needs a Roadmap to Good Governance?

Your organization may not match any of these nonprofits well. You may be on the board of a large hospital, a small museum, or a medium-sized boys and girls club. Your organization may have a staff comprising several hundred paid professionals or a handful of unpaid volunteers. You may be governing a mature organization or one that is just starting up. Your reach may be the world or simply your neighborhood. Your organization may be dedicated to growth or content to serve at its existing level. Whatever the profile of your organization, it deserves good governance—and the roadmap can get you there.

"What about 'working boards'?" we are often asked. "Our organization is a decent size, but we don't have staff, and we rely on the board members to conduct the programs, do the fundraising, even keep the books. We aren't a 'governing board' that needs to worry about the role of the board, the role of the CEO (which we don't have), or policies for this and that. Our board governs by doing."

Our response is that all boards are "governing boards" in that they share the same fiduciary responsibility for their organization. A working board is a governing board whose members *also* carry out some or all of its activities. Perhaps we can illustrate this more clearly by demonstrating the different roles that board members can play by using a simple analogy.

The Three Hats of Nonprofit Board Members

Figure 1-1 describes three "hats" that may be worn by nonprofit board members, a hat being a symbol of the role that the board member is playing at the time. The first of these is the governance hat, which is worn only when the board member is attending a board meeting or committee meeting. All board decisions are made while wearing this hat. This is the hat that you are wearing when you are looked at by the IRS and the state in which your organization is registered. These and any other regulatory agencies hold you accountable for how well you serve in your governance role.

Imagine that there's a hook on the door of your boardroom that holds another hat. When you as a board member walk out of a board meeting, you exchange your governance hat for your volunteer hat, which is essentially what you wear whenever you are outside board or committee meetings. In addition to your

FIGURE 1.1.   The Three Hats Board Members Wear.

1. Governance Hat (only hat that carries legal authority to govern)	▶ Worn only when in a properly called board or committee meeting with a quorum ▶ Decisions made only when part of the group wearing this hat ▶ CEO is accountable only to governing policies set by the board
2. Volunteer Hat (this hat carries no legal authority)	▶ Goes on when leaving a board or committee meeting ▶ Worn when advising the CEO ▶ Worn when fundraising ▶ Worn when helping staff (alone or in a group) and often under the supervision of the staff
3. Implementer Hat (carries limited authority, but is seldom worn in most boards)	▶ Seldom worn because staff usually implement board policies ▶ But worn when a board resolution or the CEO gives a board member authority to implement some board action ▶ Hat is removed when task is done

board duties, you may very well be a resource for the CEO and the staff, possibly providing personal counsel, offering a particular expertise, or just generally helping out. If you are a board member for an organization that has few staff members, you may find yourself volunteering often. Regardless, if you are not in a board meeting or a committee meeting, you are wearing your volunteer hat. And rather than the CEO working for you, as a volunteer, you are working for the CEO or her staff.

How about the third hat—the implementer hat? This is a variation on the volunteer hat in that the board member is serving in a direct staff role, not a governing role. The distinction here is that a board member wears an implementer hat when he is carrying out a specific task that the board has authorized him to do. For example, a board member wears the volunteer hat when he is helping the CEO in fund-raising, but let's say that the board appoints her, by board resolution, to actually be in charge of fund-raising because there is no one else to do it. For that specific task, the board member would be wearing an implementer hat.

For board members who essentially serve as the staff for their organization, it is important that they know what role they are playing at any given time. They work together as a governing board, then function more independently to implement the board's policies.

In summary, all nonprofit boards have the responsibility to govern. Some boards may require more of their board members, but none should require less. And it's that governance function that is the focus of the roadmap. Because all boards have a duty to govern, and because our roadmap serves the governance function, we believe that the roadmap applies to all nonprofits, regardless of their budget, size of staff, or complexity of operations. In other words, whether a nonprofit has many staff or no staff, at least the board members need to learn how to govern.

The next question is, how does one measure the quality of governance in a nonprofit organization? Further, is there a continuum along which a board can move its governance from good to great? There are several definitions of "good governance," which it may be helpful to explore before getting directly into the roadmap.

Defining "Good to Great" in the Nonprofit World

*I do not consider myself an expert on the social sectors, but . . .
I've become a passionate student. I've come to see that it is simply*

*not good enough to focus solely on having a great business sector.
If we only have great companies, we will merely have a prosperous
society, not a great one. Economic growth and power are the
means, not the definition, of a great nation.*[1]

Jim Collins

Over the past decade, few books have enjoyed the success of *Good
to Great*, the immensely readable, valuable work by Jim Collins.
The credibility of the book stems largely from a straightforward
and robust technique for (1) defining "great" and (2) identifying
those characteristics that great companies have in common. In describing the behaviors and characteristics of great companies, Collins uses catchy metaphors such as Hedgehogs and Flywheels as
well as memorable labels such as Level 5 Leadership and BHAG
(Big Hairy Audacious Goals). These terms have become part of the
vocabulary in business classrooms and boardrooms. They have
also served as reference points and rallying cries for leaders who
seek the long-term performance results of the "great" companies.

Further, the Good to Great concepts were instructive to more
than those in the private sector. It wasn't long before leaders, writers, and consultants dealing with nonprofit organizations began
applying them to nonprofit issues and situations.[2] Four years after
Good to Great, Collins published *Good to Great and the Social
Sectors*, a monograph about relating the Good to Great concepts
to nonbusiness organizations. He was prompted to write the
monograph because he estimated that:

> somewhere between 30% and 50% of those who have read *Good
> to Great* come from nonbusiness . . . education, healthcare,
> churches, the arts, social services, cause-driven nonprofits, police,
> government agencies, and even military units.[3]

He goes on to say that it will be another decade before research
similar to his study will support a definition of *great* in the social
sector; but he adds:

> In the meantime, I feel a responsibility to respond to the questions
> raised by those who seek to apply the good-to-great principles
> today and I offer this monograph as a small interim step.

The remainder of his monograph is a thoughtful application of his Good-to-Great concepts to the social sector. He illustrates how the same principles that characterize great for-profit companies can work for nonprofit organizations—even though Collins is careful not to claim that applying these principles will guarantee the same degree of performance improvement as he saw in the private sector.

Good-to-Great Governance?

The application of metrics to an organization's performance in the marketplace is one thing, but how does one go about measuring performance in the boardroom? In the Good-to-Great study of for-profit companies, the implication is that the leadership of the board and of the organization is often indistinguishable, and rightly so, as it is common practice in the private sector for the CEO of the company to also be the chair of the board.[4] Therefore, as helpful as the Good-to-Great model is in giving us sound principles of leadership and organizational behavior, even in the nonprofit world, it offers little advice on nonprofit governance. We may learn from Collins what will lead to organizational excellence, but we are left on our own as to what will lead to excellence in governance, either in the for-profit or in the nonprofit world.

Nor are we given much encouragement from studies that are designed to answer the specific question of which model or checklist of actions is the most effective form of governance for a nonprofit organization. For example, a few years ago, an academic study summarized its finding this way:

> Having reviewed the normative and academic literatures on governance in the not-for-profit organizations we conclude that there is no consensus about an ideal way of governing nonprofit organizations.[5]

Good Governance? Who Says So?

While there is no magic meter that will give us a reliable reading of quality of governance in the nonprofit sector, there is no shortage of material suggesting how to conduct an evaluation of a non-profit board. Books, articles, and web sites abound with advice on how to improve nonprofit governance. Most of the material on evaluating governance, however, consists of lists of best practices. For example, two organizations that are well known and respected in the field of nonprofit governance are:

> *Governance Matters*, formerly the Alliance for Nonprofit Governance (ANG), which serves nonprofit organizations in the New York City area with the objective of improving board governance by fostering an open exchange of ideas and information among a broad cross section of the nonprofit community

> *BoardSource*, formerly the National Center for Nonprofit Boards, which is dedicated to increasing the effectiveness of nonprofit organizations by strengthening their boards of directors

Each of these organizations has developed a list of principles or indicators of nonprofit governance quality, which are summarized in Figures 1-2 and 1-3. Like so many consultants in the field

FIGURE 1.2.   Twelve Principles of Governance that Power Exceptional Boards.*

1. Constructive Partnership
2. Mission Driven
3. Strategic Thinking
4. Culture of Inquiry
5. Independent Mindedness
6. Ethos of transparency
7. Compliance with Integrity
8. Sustaining Resources
9. Results Oriented
10. Intentional Board Practices
11. Continuous Learning
12. Revitalization

*BoardSource, *Twelve Principles of Governance That Power Exceptional Boards* (BoardSource: Washington, DC, 2005): website = www.board source.org

FIGURE 1.3.   Nonprofit Governance Indicator Guide.*

1. Board Effectiveness (5)
2. Board Operations (8)
3. Strategic Planning (4)
4. Program Effectiveness (4)
5. Stability of Funding Base (5)
6. Financial Oversight (7)
7. Constituent Representation (2)
8. External Relations (4)
9. Evaluation of the Organization's Operations and Impact (2)

*Taken from the following page of the Governance Matters® web site
http://governance1.web132.discountasp.net/web/NGIG/print.aspx
The purpose of the list is to assist grant makers as they assess the quality of
nonprofits that may be seeking grants for their organizations. The numbers
in parentheses show the indicators of good governance that are listed
under each of the nine main categories.*

of nonprofit governance, Bob has developed and refined his own
list (shown in Figure 1-4), which we call the "Attributes of Excellence."

While there are numerous similar lists from other organizations and publications, these three demonstrate what all these lists
seem to have in common, i.e., they recite what good boards do. To
illustrate this point, let's look at the BoardSource example and
read some of the statements that BoardSource makes concerning
its list of principles. In the preamble to its booklet entitled *The
Source: Twelve Principles of Governance That Power Exceptional
Boards (The Source)*, BoardSource offers this encouragement:
"Follow these 12 principles and advance the common good with
uncommonly good work." The editors go on in the preamble to
cite actions and behaviors of boards that they consider exemplary
and then ask, "How does a board rise to this [high] level? Are
there standards that describe this height of performance?"

To answer these questions, BoardSource turned to a panel of
experts, who drew on their collective experience and arrived at
twelve principles that, in their view, characterize high-performing
boards. As shown in Figure 1-2, these principles are written at a
high, somewhat conceptual level, and even BoardSource calls them
"aspirational." To help bring these principles to a more practical

FIGURE 1.4. Attributes of Excellence in Nonprofit Governance.

An excellent Board commits to:

1. **Work with the CEO** so that the board and CEO do not compete. Rather they serve separate, complementary roles and function as partners in a trust relationship.
2. **Adopt a clear mission**, which it supplements with the values and strategies to accomplish its mission.
3. **Select a CEO who is equipped to advance the mission** within board established policy parameters. Then the board governs in ways that support, compensate, evaluate and, if necessary, terminate the CEO, keeping the best interests of the organization in mind.
4. **Elect a chair** who is able and willing to manage the board and to maintain the integrity of the structure and process that the whole board has determined is best, leaving management to the CEO.
5. **Define the criteria for new members;** then select, orient, train, evaluate, and reward board service for those who give their time, talent, and treasure.
6. **Govern through policies** documented in a well-organized Board Policies Manual (BPM) of 15–20 pages, which is constantly improved as the board learns and adjusts to changing internal and external factors.
7. **Form committees** that speak *to* the board, not *for* the board and that do board-related work rather than supervise or advise staff on their work.
8. **Insist on great meetings**, which include good staff material in advance, time for social interaction and learning, and agendas that are focused on improving the BPM. Oral reports are limited to allow at least half the meeting time for board dialogue.
9. **Be accountable** through legal, financial, and program audits; observance of the law; avoidance of conflicts of interest; assessment of results; self-evaluation of the board as a whole and of individual board members; and appropriate transparency in dealing with its stakeholders.
10. **Pursue excellence** by keeping board members forward-looking and focused on outcomes/results, on disciplining themselves, and on effectual change so that they recognize, appreciate, and enjoy the process of governance.

level, each of them is broken down into two segments: (1) how responsible boards practice the principle, and (2) what these boards use as a source of power. For example, a responsible board that practiced the principle of constructive partnership would (1) "delegate operations to the chief executive" and (2) use "trust, candor, and respect" as a source of power. The outcome would be a board that "faces and resolves problems early," which, according to the panel of experts, is one of several characteristics of exceptional boards.[6]

This last point illustrates how difficult research can be in the nonprofit world. At the end of the day, even the BoardSource panel of experts is left with a framework where its conclusion rests on its own consensus definition. An "exceptional board," the panel says, is, well, one that does exceptional things—like "faces and resolves problems early."

Authors' Note: As this book was going to press, the Advisory Committee on Self-Regulation of the Charitable Sector, which was formed at the behest of the United States Senate, issued for public comment a draft report that listed 29 principles of effective practice for charitable organizations. A full copy of the report was published on the council's web site http://www.nonprofitpanel.org/participants/selfregulation/.

While the 29 principles offer more detail on what the Advisory Council considers good governance, they cover much of the same ground as the best practice lists that we describe in this chapter. We do not anticipate that the 29 principles will be materially modified as a result of public comments. Because of the relevance of the principles to our discussion, the gravitas of the council, the timeliness of the publication, and the likely exposure that the list will receive in the nonprofit community, we have posted a list of the 29 principles on the AMA website (see Appendix B).

It's Not So Much the What as the How

While academics may prefer the data-supported rigor of *Good to Great*, there is still much we can learn from lists of best practices in nonprofit governance. We believe, for instance, that all three lists mentioned here—Governance Matters's indicators, Board-Source's principles, and our attributes—are excellent points of reference against which to compare a nonprofit board. And remember that these are only three of scores of such lists, many of which would also be valuable for measuring quality in governance.

No, our concern is not so much with the lack of definition of "great" or "exceptional" boards, but rather with how one moves into that category, i.e., how a nonprofit board goes from good to great. To be fair to BoardSource and most of the other publications listing best practices in the nonprofit sector, the purpose of *The Source* is to list the twelve principles, not to tell people how to implement them. And perhaps BoardSource was thinking about the "how" when it published *The Nonprofit Policy Sampler (Policy Sampler)*, which is:

> Designed to help nonprofit leaders—board and staff—advance their organizations, make better collective decisions, and guide individual actions and behaviors.[7]

The *Policy Sampler* is a reference book that discusses how board policies can be developed in some forty-nine different areas of nonprofit governance, which are assembled into eight different categories. The book comes with a CD of sample policies that can be tailored to a board's particular situation. It is an effective reference that will be useful to nonprofit leaders who want some help in drafting policies. In the end, however, the *Policy Sampler* goes only partway in moving the nonprofit board from good to great.

In its preface, the *Policy Sampler* says that:

> The major policies of a nonprofit organization are created and ratified by its board of directors, are (or should be) written down in a policy manual for easy reference, are (or should be) reviewed

frequently to see if they are up to date, and cover every aspect of the organization's business.[8]

The parenthetical comments "or should be" are not ours, although we certainly support their insertion and we wholeheartedly agree with the overall statement. In fact, it does well to describe the premise for the book you are now reading, because while the *Policy Sampler* gives plenty of good advice on how to write policies, it offers little guidance on how to develop a policy manual. In a sense, it is a list of ingredients without the recipe to show how the ingredients go together. If we were asked to edit the preceding quote from the *Policy Sampler*, we would say:

A nonprofit organization can move its governance from good to great if its board of directors develops policies that cover every aspect of the organization's business and documents them in a Board Policies Manual that it reviews at every board meeting and updates frequently.

The operative term in our amended quote is "Board Policies Manual" (BPM), which, as we will explain in the rest of this book, is the key element in a plan to implement best practices in nonprofit governance. A BPM will never have the glamor of Collins's BHAG, but if it's incorporated into the roadmap that we lay out in Chapter 2, nothing we know of is more efficient in moving a nonprofit board from good to great.

The Board Policies Manual: Your Essential Guide

Figure 2-1 depicts the roadmap to good governance. At first glance (and probably second and third glance as well), this map is unlikely to increase your heart rate or motivate you to embark on such an uninspiring journey. Our challenge in this book is to provide that motivation by demonstrating why the roadmap offers the most direct route to good governance.

The journey laid out in Figure 2-1 comprises three segments or legs, each involving the Board Policies Manual (BPM):

First leg: Committing to the BPM
Second leg: Developing the BPM
Third leg: Integrating the BPM.

Obviously, a prerequisite to understanding the roadmap is understanding the BPM: what it is, why it is, and how it is used. Before exploring each of the segments of the roadmap, therefore, we describe the BPM and discuss why we believe that it is the highway to good governance.

FIGURE 2-1.   The Roadmap to Good Governance.

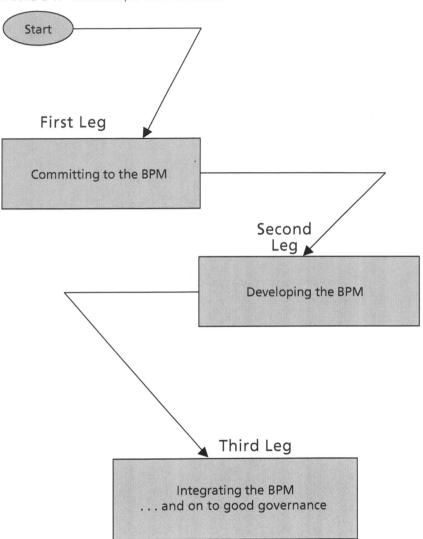

What Is the BPM?

The BPM is a document—really an organized booklet with a specific outline of topics—that contains *all* the critical standing (ongoing) policies that any board needs to address. The BPM represents the voice of the board to the CEO, the staff, and other stakeholders of the organization. Because boards are supposed to think and act strategically, its policies are typically written from a fairly high level—we like to say 5,000 feet. (Higher than that would be *too* high, preventing the board from seeing essential features below.) The size of a BPM can range from several pages to twenty pages long, with most BPMs somewhere around fifteen to seventeen pages. The length is dependent on how specific the board wants to be with respect to the number of policies and their level of detail. However, even though it is constantly updated, we recommend that your BPM be no longer than 20 pages. Appendix A contains a template of the BPM that we will use throughout this book to illustrate how the BPM is put together and how you can tailor your BPM to fit your organization.

The BPM in the Hierarchy of Board Documents

Among the documents generated by or for an organization, we like to say that the BPM is in Box 5, as shown in Figure 2-2. Most boards are not obligated to function under the authority of a parent organization, although that is common with certain church denominations and national organizations that have state and local subsidiaries. Unless you are one of those, Box 2 in Figure 2-2 would not apply. The articles of incorporation (Box 3) is the legal document filed with a secretary of state that establishes the organization as a nonprofit corporation and therefore subject to the laws of that state. It can be changed by board action, but the changes must then be approved by the secretary of state for the state in which it is incorporated. Because the articles define the purpose of the organization and the primary constituents to be served in high-level terms, that document seldom needs changing.

The bylaws (Box 4) define the authority of the governing board, its size, how it is organized, a description of the officers' roles, and related matters. Bylaws are typically filed with the IRS and the secretary of state. While they may be amended frequently, we recommend that bylaws be written to reflect only the essentials that are infrequently changed, leaving to the BPM the definition of roles, structures, and processes that are more likely to be modified

FIGURE 2.2.   Hierarchy of Organizational Policies.*

1. FEDERAL AND STATE LAWS (A board expects staff to monitor)
2. Parent Organization Policies (Does not apply to all non-profits)
3. Articles of Incorporation (Seldom needs changing)
4. By-Laws (Should be revised and updated regularly)
5. BOARD POLICIES MANUAL (BPM) (The "one-voice" of the board in an evolving, comprehensive document of 15–20 pages)
6. CEO-LEVEL POLICIES (Planning documents, personnel manual etc.)
7. OTHER ORGANIZATIONAL POLICIES (Often determined in and by various staff units)

Advancement	Communications	Finance	Programs	Etc.

*Each level is consistent with those above.

to reflect changing realities. Good bylaws can be as few as ten to twelve pages. In a membership organization, the bylaws usually constitute the message from the members to the board as to their expectations for the board. As such, the bylaws in a member organization can normally be changed only by a vote of the members. In a few member organizations and in most organizations without a well-defined membership, the board is authorized to amend the bylaws, a step that typically requires advance notice and that may require an approval by a supermajority vote, i.e., a two-thirds or three-quarters vote of the board.

Skipping over Box 5 in Figure 2-2 for the moment, Box 6 represents the policies and procedures that exist within the organization to provide efficiency and fairness in its operations. These documents may include a personnel manual, accounting procedures, a staff operations plan, and any number of other important "policies and procedures" that guide staff members in their day-to-day work. The extent of these operational documents tends to vary with the size and complexity of the organization and with the degree to which uniformity is desired or required. A hospital, for example, is likely to have extensive detail on operational matters, while a tightly focused charitable organization may not.

Regardless of the extent of the operational or organizational policies and procedures, the board will have little involvement in their development, since developing and maintaining them is essentially within the purview of the CEO. However, the board does have an interest in these varied documents in Box 6, and most board members want to influence them in general terms. The proper approach is to use the BPM to speak to whatever the board wants to address at a higher level than the Box 6 documents. For example, the board may require in its BPM that the personnel manual include a grievance process for employees or a clear statement of nondiscrimination. It may also require that a certain accounting treatment be used for specific transactions and be incorporated in the accounting manual.

Here are the two key principles: (1) The board speaks with one voice in its BPM and does not try to write documents that are better left to staff, and (2) the content of each box in Figure 2-2 must not violate the content (policies) in the boxes above it. The policies in the BPM, therefore, must be consistent with the bylaws, the articles of incorporation, the law, and so on. Normally, a board looks to its CEO and to its board governance committee to monitor compliance. Likewise, the many operational policies approved by the CEO—or by senior executives reporting to him—must conform to the board policies in the BPM and the documents above Box 5. All this will become clearer as we proceed.

Content and Organization of the BPM

When we say that the BPM contains all the standing policies that the board needs to address, we mean those policies that are ongoing in nature. In that sense, therefore, the BPM is not a record of all board decisions. To highlight this point, note in Figure 2-3 how we distinguish board "policies" from routine and periodic board "decisions."

We organize the BPM into five parts. Although we do not change the number and purpose of these parts, the content contained in each part is always under review and is always refined by board action as the board adjusts to realities and becomes wiser in its governance leadership. Briefly, here is a description of each part.

BPM Part 1: Introduction and Administration

Because most people are not familiar with the BPM, few first-time board members and other readers will know exactly what to expect from the document. Accordingly, it is important to give them a clear explanation of both what the BPM is and what it isn't. Part 1 of the BPM states the purpose of the BPM, how it is maintained, who is responsible for the different parts and subparts, and how it is employed in the governance model for the organization. Because it is important to understand the purpose and the context of the BPM (Part 1), we put it right up front. Once the board is comfortable with its description of the purpose and maintenance of its BPM in Part 1, it may not amend this part again.

BPM Part 2: Organization Essentials

One of the principles of a nonprofit board is to think strategically. In BPM Part 2, the board has the opportunity to put its mark and blessing on the strategic direction of the organization. There are libraries full of books about how to write a vision and mission statement, how to set and maintain core values, and how to develop a strategic plan. However, as the board decides to handle what we call the *organization essentials*, the wisdom and clarity reflected in them become the heart and character of the organization's work. This Part 2 is the foundation upon which the organization's other policies are designed.

In addition to the important statements about vision, mission,

FIGURE 2.3.   Two Types of Votes by Nonprofit Boards.

BOARD DECISIONS (kept in minutes)	BOARD POLICIES (kept in BPM)
* Proposed by CEO or board members	* Proposed by CEO or board members
* Determined by board vote	* Determined by board vote
* Kept in board minutes that should be filed over the life of organization	* Ideally kept in Board Policies Manual (BPM) [15–20 pages]
* Usually short-term application of the decision	* Could be on-going for years
* Changed little, if any, when approved at next meeting	* Changed as often as new data convince board it should be changed
* Usually unrelated to Bylaws	* Must never conflict with Bylaws (or Articles or government rules)
* Of limited use in orienting new board members	* BPM is an essential document for orienting new board members
* Little need to refer back to minutes after a year or so	* Important to review/update BPM at every meeting
Examples of Board Decisions	*Examples of Board Policies*
- Approve an agenda	- Adopt mission, values, strategies
- Approve a financial report	- Adopt major goals
- Approve previous minutes	- Define committees and make-up
- Appoint or terminate a CEO	- Criteria for new board members
- Elect a board member or officer	- Evaluation process for CEO
- Adopt a budget	- Guidelines for finances
- Approve a new program	- Limitations on program activities
- Pass resolution of commendation	- Parameters around fundraising

values, and so on that are included in this part, we also recommend that it contain the current organizational goals and priorities for at least the next twelve to eighteen months. These current goals are often proposed by the CEO, but the board's formal adoption of them allows the CEO and the board to align their expectations, and constitutes a basis on which the CEO will be evaluated by the board. Having the current goals in this part puts them in the strategic context, i.e., it allows them to be viewed alongside the other organization essentials to ensure that all board and executive actions are in line with the strategic direction.

BPM Part 3: Board Structure and Process

This part explains how the board is configured and how it operates. It includes such features as:

- Governance style, e.g., outward looking, strategic thinking, speaking with one voice
- Board job description, e.g., principal functions, scope of action
- Board membership, e.g., the board's size, qualifications of members, term of office, election process, rules for removal
- Officers, e.g., their responsibilities, terms of office, election process, rules for removal
- Committees, e.g., number and type, scope of responsibilities, selection of members, relationship with staff, expectation of members
- Advisors and task forces, e.g., authority for forming, role in governance process

Many of these features are covered in the organization's bylaws at some level. For example, in a membership organization, the members will typically determine the size of the board, the terms of the board members, the election process, and other related features. In almost every case, however, the bylaws are silent on important specifics. For example, they may specify that committee members are appointed by the chair, but not address the terms of those appointments or who selects committee chairs. We prefer, actually, that bylaws be lean and that specific structure and process decisions be left to board members whenever they agree on changes to the BPM. To eliminate confusion on these matters, some bylaw provisions can be repeated in the BPM in the context of providing a succinct but full explanation of a given topic. Doing so prevents having to jump back and forth between the BPM and the bylaws.

BPM Part 4: Board–CEO/Staff Relationship

The most important relationship for organization effectiveness is that between the board and the CEO. A lack of clarity on their respective roles and how the board and the CEO will interact almost ensures frustration on the part of both parties. It is surprising, therefore, that so many nonprofit organizations have not documented how the board and the CEO will work together. Part 4 includes not only everything that the board needs to say about its relationship with its one agent, the chief executive, but also what it wants to say about the staff in general. These issues will all be discussed in more detail later on, but here are the typical topics addressed in this part:

- How authority is conveyed from the board to the CEO
- What is expected of the CEO overall
- How, when, and by whom the CEO will be evaluated
- How, when, and what the CEO communicates with board members
- Guidance on how the CEO is to employ and treat staff
- What happens when the CEO resigns or is asked to leave

Although this part is sometimes viewed by the CEO as restrictive and bureaucratic, our experience is that once the content of this part is agreed upon by the board after strong consideration of the CEO's views, its clarity will add to the trust of the board and do more to free up the CEO than to restrict her. These rules are as valuable to the CEO in "managing up" as they are to the board in "delegating down."

BPM Part 5: Executive Parameters

This part provides more specific guidance from the board to the CEO on the major functional areas of the organization. The CEO is the single agent of the board, and the CEO is responsible for managing the organization within the parameters set by the board.

A common concern of the staff of a nonprofit is micromanagement from the board. The flip side of that view is the board concern that the staff may not be operating according to its sense of prudent management. A resolution between these views can be achieved when the board documents the policies that it wants the staff to follow and then leaves to the CEO the responsibility of determining more detailed policies and monitoring compliance with those policies (Boxes 6 and 7 in Figure 2-2).

Often the policies in this part are expressed as limitations, e.g., limits on spending, program expansion, hours of operation, or service delivery. Although most of the policies in this part do serve to limit the CEO, we prefer the less negative label of setting parameters for executive actions, whether the statements indicate what the board wants done or what it does not want done. Again, while some CEOs and staff are at first leery about any limitations on their decision authority, having clear parameters concerning finances, major programs, fund-raising, and other such areas actually frees them up to make professional judgments day after day within the parameters without fear of being second-guessed by the board later on. After the board speaks to these issues, it must free the staff to move ahead without hesitation or fear of being criticized for making decisions.

Benefits of the BPM

Strategic Benefits of the BPM

We state in this book that, in our experience, developing a BPM is the most direct way for a nonprofit board to improve the way it governs an organization. While we are comfortable with that assertion, we can also draw on research other than our experience to demonstrate that following the roadmap in this book will produce benefits for the board that are wide and deep.

For almost two decades, John Carver has been one of the most influential voices in nonprofit governance.[1] His research and writings on the Policy Governance model have been groundbreaking, and many of the principles that are reflected in this book are taken from Carver's work. In his seminal book *Boards That Make a Difference*, he identifies three basic products or contributions of the nonprofit board that it cannot delegate. He calls them "the irreducible minimum contributions of governance."[2] They are:

- *Linkage to the ownership.* Connecting the moral owners with the organization.
- *Explicit governing policies.* Expressing the values and perspectives of the organization in explicitly enunciated and properly catalogued policies.
- *Assurance of organizational performance.* Ensuring organizational performance that is consistent with applicable policies.

We see the BPM as speaking directly to each of these essential contributions of the board.

- Linkage to the ownership: The BPM includes clear statements of the organization's purpose, including its mission, vision, and values. It identifies the stakeholders and acknowledges the role of the board in serving them. It articulates the major goals of the organization in the near and medium term and outlines the strategy to reach its goals.

- Explicit governing policies: The BPM is the single source for all standing board policies, written in clear language and structured for ease of understanding by board members, staff members, and other stakeholders.

- Assurance of organizational performance: The BPM dedicates Part 4 to the board–CEO relationship, including the basis for the board's evaluation of the CEO, the process that the board will use, and the shared expectations that the board and the CEO have for each other. BPM Part 4 also makes it clear that the CEO's performance is synonymous with the organization's performance. Finally, BPM Part 4 lays out the reports that the board will use to monitor performance.

Mapping the features of the BPM to Carver's irreducible contributions of the board testifies to the BPM's value at a macro level of governance. The BPM is not just a neat tool that boards will find helpful in streamlining their activities. It is an authentic strategic governance action that speaks to the essentials of the board's role and responsibilities.

Tactical Benefits of the BPM

For all the support at the macro level for developing a BPM, there is no shortage of support at what we call the tactical level. Here are several benefits of the BPM that boards have found.

The Board Speaks with One Voice. The bylaws of a nonprofit organization usually describe its board in general terms. It's up to the board to add detail to the bylaws in terms of both structure and process, i.e., how the board will be organized and how it will carry out its responsibilities. Although in the eyes of the state the organization is a "person," the board, unlike an individual person, comprises many personalities and perspectives. It must deal with perhaps as many views as it has board members, and too often its communications sound like a cacophony rather than a clear statement. The solution is not to ensure that a board is homogeneous, i.e., that all its members think alike. Quite the contrary. Good boards contain and accommodate a diversity of perspectives and thoughts. They give time and respect to individual differences, and they are rewarded with a message that the board as a whole can support. Although there may be discussion, even vociferous debate, of competing viewpoints in a board meeting, when the board finally speaks to an issue in the form of policy, it should speak with one voice. The BPM ensures that the board's voice is clear, consistent, and current. This is the primary benefit of the BPM.

Policies Are Explicit. All boards have policies, which are revealed in the decisions they make and the actions they take. Some of the policies are explicit (written down). Others are only implicit (unwritten). The problem with unwritten policies is twofold: First, they may be known by only a few individuals within and outside the board, and second, these implicit policies are given by those in the know as reasons why explicit (written) policies are not needed. Articulating all standing policies in a concise, well-thumbed document provides an easy reference both for board members and for the CEO and the staff so that they know at all times on what matters the board has spoken.

Efficiency of Having Board Policies in One Place. Boards are required to prepare minutes of their meetings, and often these minutes will reflect policy decisions. Executive committees are usually authorized to create certain policies, and the minutes of their meetings may also contain policy statements. Therefore, the board's voice may be distributed over several years of minutes of board meetings and executive committee meetings. Anyone who has waded through the minutes of past board meetings to decipher policy resolutions will appreciate the efficiency of having to look in only one place—the BPM.

Efficient Orientation of New Board Members. One consistent criticism that we hear from new board members is that they lack confidence in assuming their new position because they are unsure of their responsibilities, what is expected of them, and how they fit into the board structure. A BPM can go a long way toward allaying those concerns and encouraging new members to be involved at an early stage of their term. A careful reading of the normal-sized BPM typically requires no more than an hour. With that investment of time, new board members can understand:

1. What is required of them
2. What they can expect from the CEO

3. Which matters the board has addressed in the past
4. What short- and intermediate-term goals have been set for the organization

Eased Policy Development and Elimination of Duplication. It is not uncommon for boards to address policies without considering their impact on policies that have already been established and that may reside in past minutes. As a result, policies are developed that either reinvent the wheel or, worse, actually conflict with current (but forgotten) policies. The most appropriate way to formulate policy is to put it in the language of the BPM and incorporate it into the relevant section. There the new policy can be put in the context of existing policies to determine how it will fit. When committees are asked to look at an issue that will find its way into board policy, their report back to the board should include the draft of the language for the BPM within the appropriate section of the BPM. Often, one board member may make a motion to do this or that, only to be reminded by another board member that the board already has a sufficient policy in place.

Clear Guidance to the CEO. There is no more important job of the board than assuring the performance of the CEO, and hence of the organization. Although this is a universally accepted axiom of governance, too many boards have either highly subjective methods for evaluating their CEOs or a process that is poorly documented or unevenly followed. The BPM makes it clear to the CEO:

- That the board owns the mission statement, as well as the key values and strategies of the organization (Part 2, Organization Essentials)
- What the board expects of itself (Part 3, Board Structure and Process)
- How the board interfaces with the CEO and the staff (Part 4, Board–CEO/Staff Relationship)
- What parameters the CEO must observe in carrying out her duties (Part 5, Executive Parameters)

Modeling Efficiency and Competence to CEO and Staff. The board has the responsibility for modeling the competence and excellence that it expects from the CEO and the staff. Working with the BPM demonstrates a commitment to clarity and transparency that sends the right signal to people inside and outside the organization. Even though the BPM is a board document, its development and ongoing maintenance typically involve a high level of input from the CEO and the staff. As they work with the board on the policies that go into the BPM, they gain an appreciation for the distinctive roles of the board and the staff and a respect for how and why the policies were developed.

The BPM and the Roadmap

Although the benefits of the BPM are well known and persuasive, we have found that too few nonprofits have a BPM, and fewer still make it an integral part of their governance process. There are many reasons for this, and we discuss several of them in Chapter 4. The fundamental reason for not developing a BPM is that boards and CEOs don't know how to do it. Indeed, a large percentage of the BPMs or similar documents being used by nonprofits have been developed by consultants. While working with consultants is one appropriate approach to developing a new BPM, the majority of nonprofits do not have large consulting budgets. That's why we wrote this book.

In the remaining chapters, we will take you through the three legs of the roadmap that are identified in Figure 2-1. In some respects, with the widespread use of modern technology such as Global Positioning Systems (GPS), *roadmap* may be an antiquated term. Today, these marvelous GPS devices can tell us exactly where we are and how to get where we are going—and even give us multiple routes to our destination.

Both of us were in the Army in the 1960s, and we remember map reading as being part of our training. Equipped with only a map and a compass, we learned to identify where we were and to plot a course to our destination. We learned how to use maps of different scales, which were measured in terms of the ratio of the distance on the map to the actual distance on the ground.

This use of multiple maps with different scales seems very cumbersome now. The new GPS devices handle scale with ease, normally offering several views, from the highest level, which may show the entire country, to the most detailed view, which gives local street names and even addresses along the streets. In a real sense, we have tried to give you the same option with our road-map, i.e., the ability to choose the scale or level of detail that applies to your board. Some of you may prefer a BPM that gives the big picture—at least initially. Others may want the detail even on early drafts of the BPM. We trust that our roadmap will afford you those options and that, despite its rather outdated label, the roadmap will be GPS-like in its flexibility and versatility across a wide range of nonprofit organizations.

CHAPTER 3

Planning and Packing: Committing to the BPM

Plans are only good intentions unless they immediately degenerate into hard work.

—Peter Drucker

We don't expect that you need to be reminded of the value of good planning in any endeavor. Nor are we worried that this message from Peter Drucker will be lost on the majority of readers. Most of us have seen plans of all sorts atrophy as a result of inattention to such an extent that they become useless. And it is a rare plan of any substance that doesn't require the hard work that Drucker sees as the key ingredient that turns good intentions into reality.

Translating Plans Into Work

Our roadmap to good governance includes a first leg that we call *commitment*, a label meant to encompass those actions necessary for gaining the support of the board and the CEO to complete the journey. The commitment, therefore, includes more than just making the investment to develop the BPM (the second leg of the journey); it also includes the intention to maintain the BPM as the voice of the board throughout the life of the organization (the third leg). To draw on the Drucker quote given at the beginning of this chapter, the commitment segment of the roadmap describes those things that must be done to move the "good intentions" of a BPM to the "hard work" of its development and subsequent integration.

Before we get into the steps of this first leg, let us acknowledge that the next several pages are written for boards that are not familiar with policy manuals for the board, whether or not they are called BPMs. What is more, you may already have passed the point of persuasion and have all the commitment that you need from your board. If you are comfortable that the board and the CEO are fully behind the development of the BPM, feel free to go directly to the second leg of the journey. Before you skip over this chapter and the next ("Confronting the Roadblocks"), however, give the points in the next several pages a quick once-over to at least satisfy yourself that you have safely passed the milestones on the way to commitment and that the key players are prepared to develop the BPM (the second leg) and follow through on its integration (the third leg).

Milestones on the Way to Commitment

Get the Board on Board

Completing this leg basically involves getting the CEO and the board, well, on board. As the voice of the board to itself, to the CEO, and to other key stakeholders, the BPM is written, owned, and updated by the board. If it isn't, writing and maintaining it are a waste of time. For some boards, particularly those that are already familiar with Carver's Policy Governance model and the principles described in Bob's book, *The Nonprofit Board Answer Book*, selling the BPM concept should be a straightforward exercise. Even in these situations, however, don't take the board's buy-in for granted.

If you or your board has worked with a consultant in the past, you may ask him to help you get the necessary commitment to develop and integrate the BPM. In our experience, of those boards that have gone on to develop a BPM, most have been prompted to do so by a consultant. A substantial percentage of our nonprofit clients have learned about the BPM during one of our workshops, and almost all of them have been convinced of its benefits. When the enthusiasm from the workshop wanes, however, only a little over half of these clients actually move on to develop the BPM. The rest of them never get past the first leg of the journey.[1]

So while you may draw on a consultant for help in the initial selling, don't take it for granted that you will eventually get your board's commitment to the BPM. As we point out in Chapter 4, there are many roadblocks that may be erected on the way to commitment. Unless you plan to use the consultant to help you through all three legs of the roadmap, don't presume that the running start your consultant may provide will be enough to enable you to complete the journey.

But we did not write this book to promote the use of consultants. Quite the opposite. We want to give you the tools and the confidence to take this journey on your own. Accordingly, what follows in the next several pages is a rather detailed description of the steps you can take to complete the first leg of the roadmap. We suggest a simple four-step process for gaining the necessary commitment from the board, a process not unlike the one you would use to present any major proposal. It assumes that you will be starting from scratch with your board and that you are not the chair or CEO. If either of these assumptions is incorrect, you can skip over the unnecessary steps and still gain the board's commitment to the development and integration of a BPM. Or, even if you are not the chair or the CEO, but you enjoy a comfortable, open relationship with those people, you may prefer to forgo Step 1 altogether, along with the more formal portions of Steps 2 through 4. In summary, we have included all the steps because we assume it will be easier for you to see where to skip a step than to add one.

1. *Lay the groundwork.* Speak informally to your board chair, CEO, and chair of the governance committee[2] about the benefits of the BPM and ask them to consider it for the organization. You may go into that meeting with the plan discussed in Step 2, or you may want to give them some time to conduct their own investigation of the value of the BPM before you make a formal request to put the BPM on the board agenda. If they ask who among the principal experts are proponents of a board policy manual, you can go to the Internet and find scores of references. Probably the two most influential sources of advice in nonprofit governance are the Carvers, John and his wife, Miriam, at www.carvergovernance .com, and BoardSource at www.boardsource.org, with its many publications, including Bob's *The Nonprofit Board Answer Book*.[3] While these references do not mention the BPM per se, they will give your chair and your CEO a good view of the depth of support for documenting board policies systematically and using them as a primary tool for governing. Another useful piece of research is to check with your colleagues on the board to see if any of them has experience with a BPM or a similar document on another board.

2. *Formalize your proposal.* Present your case for a BPM to a subgroup of the board, perhaps the governance committee. Here we recommend that you give a presentation similar to the one that you expect to give to the full board.[4] Although it may seem like overkill for the subgroup, giving a full rehearsal will allow you to get feedback on how the entire presentation comes across. Moreover, the members of that subgroup may well be the most influential members of the board, especially if they are on the governance committee. Their support during the board meeting will be invaluable to the success of your proposal. In fact, if you find enthusiastic support, perhaps the governance committee would be willing to bring the proposal to the board as a committee recommendation. Because the chair and the CEO are usually the agenda setters, the

goal of the meeting with the subgroup is not only to secure their support, but also to secure a place on the next agenda that is of sufficient length to contain your presentation and the substantial amount of discussion that normally ensues. Depending on the size of the board and the degree of resistance to the concept that you expect, we recommend a slot on the agenda of at least two hours.

3. *Refine your proposal.* Once your proposal is on the agenda, you can turn your attention to selling the board on the BPM concept. You probably will have recommended changes arising from your meetings and discussions in Step 2. After you have made those changes, think about what may be helpful in preparing the board members for your proposal. Some boards have effective protocols for sending out materials prior to board meetings. If so, you obviously want to conform to this pattern. If there is some flexibility as to what you can send out ahead of the board meeting, we recommend a pre-mailing of material that will alert the board members to your proposal and the rationale for including it on the agenda. You may want to lift material from Chapter 2 of this book, where we describe the BPM and its benefits. You may also want to refer the board members to other references that you have used (see Step 1). As with the earlier group to whom you presented the concept, you may find that only a few board members do much research on their own, but giving them the opportunity to do so will add credibility to your proposal and offer the more diligent members an added source of research.

4. *Present to the board.* As suggested earlier, you may be comfortable with less formality in Steps 1 through 3 than is suggested here. You may be the chair or the CEO, and so you may feel that you can make the decision to move ahead with the BPM without full board discussion; however, as we discuss in Chapter 4, there may well be roadblocks thrown up along the path, and the more deliberate you are in preparing the board for a decision, the more likely you are to sell the concept. If the skids have been properly greased, your presentation to the board should be a logical extension of your preparation, premeeting conversations, premeeting mailings, and follow-up communications with your board mem-

bers. If you need a visual of a BPM to hand out at the meeting, use our template that is displayed fully in Appendix A and available for downloading (see Appendix B). Also available for downloading is a generic presentation to the board. The presentation is in PowerPoint format and included on the list in Appendix B.

Appendix B contains a presentation that you may want to tailor to your situation. It too can be downloaded from the web site.

In your presentation, be sure to emphasize the decision that you want from the board. And remember, as the pig realized when the chicken suggested that they prepare ham and eggs for the farmer's breakfast, for him it's not just a decision—it's a commitment. Don't let the board members perceive their resolution as anything less. They need to know that not only will they be involved in the development of the BPM, but they will also be expected to make it an ongoing focal point of the governance model for the organization. Following the presentation, ask for a formal vote from the board on developing a BPM, including an approval of the process and a timetable for its development. Include also the commitment of the members to review drafts and to offer clear, constructive feedback on early drafts and revisions. The board does not need to be unanimous in this decision (although it often is), but you need to get a clear consensus of support in the vote. A bare majority normally does not translate into a commitment, and not only will your development effort be more onerous without a commitment up front, but you could be faced with an uneven integration of the BPM as you try to make it the centerpiece of your governance model.

✧

This segment of the roadmap probably looks smooth and straightforward. It can be negotiated without incident, and we don't want to exaggerate the effort necessary to get on to the second (development) leg of the journey. But getting the board to the point where it is ready to make a commitment is rarely without its potential roadblocks, which we describe and discuss in Chapter 4.

CHAPTER 4

Confronting the Roadblocks

There is nothing more difficult to carry out, nor more doubtful of success, nor more dangerous to handle than to initiate a new order of things. For the reformer has enemies in all who profit by the old order, and only luke-warm defenders in all those who would profit by the new order. This luke-warmness arises partly from fear of their adversaries, who have the law in their favor, and partly from incredulity of mankind, who do not truly believe in anything new until they have had actual experience of it.

—Machiavelli, *The Prince* (1513)

Most people are in favor of progress. It's just the changes that they don't like.

—Anonymous

Notwithstanding the many advantages of the BPM, only a small percentage of nonprofits have developed a BPM and employed it fully as an integral part of their governance function. There are many reasons for this, and if you are thinking about following our roadmap, you can be fairly sure that you will run into roadblocks similar to those discussed in this chapter.

37

Vive la Resistance

Whether or not you put the reaction to change in Machiavellian terms, you have probably experienced the natural resistance to change in your organization. The changes brought about by developing a BPM will range from modest to extensive, depending on the organization, but you can be sure that following the roadmap in this book will require adjustments in the governance process. And these adjustments are not short-term. They are permanent. The goal is not simply to have a nice neat document to put on your shelf, but rather to establish a framework for improvements across the entire governance function. Yes, a completed document (BPM) lies at the end of the road, but the real objective is a changed board mindset, not just a new manual. Some people compare a board's switch to a BPM-centric approach to changing its "governance operating system." Although this comparison is valid up to a point, it may not convey the full impact of adopting the BPM. This is not simply like a PC user learning to use a Mac operating system. Integrating the BPM into your governance framework requires significantly more adjustment for boards than merely changing computer systems.

In some respects, we welcome some of the discomfort or even outright resistance that may greet the concept of a BPM. Such expressions often mean that those registering the concern understand the impact that the BPM can have on an organization. In addressing the roadblocks, we have found that not only can we allay the fears of those who question the BPM's value, but we can also underscore the benefits of the BPM in the process.

We list here several of the reasons we have heard why the BPM is not appropriate for a nonprofit. In almost every case, these concerns about the value of the BPM are well intentioned, logical, and given in the spirit of constructive input. Our rather terse commentary on these concerns is meant to deal with the substance of each complaint and not to assume that the complaint was intended to be disruptive or self-serving. With all due respect to Machiavelli, who may be more inclined to question motives, we believe that the case for developing a BPM stands on its merits, and we recommend that in selling and defending the effort, you stay on the high road.

We Don't Want to Develop a BPM Because . . .

"Our Governance Isn't Broke, and We Don't Need to Fix It"

Many boards believe that their policies are well known and that documenting those policies would be a waste of time. They believe that their board members know the policies and that they have had few problems that required new resolutions or policies. These boards feel that their members would view the document as bureaucratic, and they don't believe that they would operate any differently anyway.

Our Response

Take a look at Figure 4-1, where we summarize a view from John Carver on the subject of implicit and explicit policies. The phe-

FIGURE 4-1. Gresham's Law Applied to Board Policy.

Bad (Implicit) Policy Drives out Good (Explicit) Policy

"Board policy can be alive but invisible. Although it is hard to find true board policy in written form, it is always possible to find it in unwritten form. Actually, it may not be found so much as suspected. Ironically, unwritten policy is sometimes thought to be so clear that no one feels the need to write it down and, at the same time, so variously interpreted as to border on being capricious. In a sense, there is never a de facto lack of policy; it always exists in the actions taken. *Implicit* policy not only fills in for missing *explicit* policy, but is even used to excuse the absence of the latter."
John Carver, *Boards That Make a Difference*

Gresham's Law in economics says that bad money drives out good money in circulation. As Carver points out above, implicit policies, in addition to causing frustration with board members and CEOs, can "drive out" explicit policies.

nomenon that Carver describes is all too common among boards. We call it a form of Gresham's Law as applied to governance. You may recall from your economics class that Gresham's Law states that bad money in an economy will drive out good money because people will spend the bad money (e.g., shaved coins) and hoard the good money, thereby taking it out of circulation. In a similar way, implicit (unwritten) policies on a board will dilute and even invalidate random explicit (written) policies. When board members realize that certain written policies adopted here and there over the years don't reflect the way things are actually done, they will no longer refer to those policies, effectively taking them "out of circulation."

Boards that govern primarily through unwritten policies normally have a steep learning curve that new members are required to climb. Sometimes the steepness of the curve is worn like a badge by the "old hands." Mounting the learning curve is considered a sort of initiation or rite of passage for new members. Unfortunately, this is too often the mentality of those who like the oral tradition, who feel safer with subjectivity, who prefer to rely on institutional memories, or who presume that the policy at any given time is whatever the board chair or the CEO says it is. This type of rationale should not be the basis for forgoing the benefits of a BPM.

Good boards are well configured. They take pains to include diverse perspectives, and they maintain a culture in which different views are heard and valued. These boards want to have all their cylinders firing—i.e., to have all of their members contributing, regardless of each member's seniority on the board. Having only those "in the know" be effective board members means that you lose the advantage of the full range of the board's skills, expertise, and perspective. Rarely is a board that is an "old boys' network" perceived as a good board or one that talented people choose to be a part of. An open, transparent board is far more likely to attract new, committed members with fresh ideas. And nothing will contribute more to that image than a well-developed BPM.

Most of us have heard the expression "we have always done it this way" and perhaps have held it out as an example of antiquated, old-school thinking. Yet that is the not-so-subtle message from those boards that rely on oral tradition as the basis for their governance. Even the claim that "we have never had any problems governing this way" is, in our view, unconvincing. Waiting until it rains to fix a leaky roof may have worked for the fiddler in Arkansas (Figure 4-2), but it's a poor mindset for a board that has clear legal and fiduciary responsibilities. Developing an effective BPM won't solve all unforeseen problems, but it will give the board better vision of problems before they arise and better tools to deal with them once they are identified.

"Our Board Is Too Small and Our Policies Too Few to Justify a BPM"

There are close to two million nonprofit boards in the United States, and a large percentage of them have budgets below $100,000. Developing a BPM may seem to be an unnecessary effort for a board with modest means and a limited scope of oversight. Even if they accept our claim that developing a BPM does not require an extraordinary investment of time and money, it is difficult for these boards to see the benefits of a BPM that would justify the effort.

Our Response

While we sympathize with this reaction, it is an extremely rare situation where developing a BPM is not worth the investment—

FIGURE 4-2.   Always a Reason Not to Fix the Roof or Not to Develop a BPM.

The traveler replied: "That's all quite true,
But this, I think, is the thing for you to do;
Get busy on a day that is fair and bright,
Then pitch the old roof till it's good and tight."

But the old man kept on playing his reel,
And tapped the ground with his leathery heel:
"Get along," said he, "for you give me a pain;
My cabin never leaks when it doesn't rain."

The Arkansas Traveler
5th & 6th verses (Composer Unknown)

even for a small board with oversight of an organization with limited reach and resources. In Chapter 2, we compare the scale of a map to the amount of detail in a BPM. If the board is small or is experiencing little or no trouble with its policies or communication, it can limit its BPM development to simply documenting the few policies and principles that are presently being used. However, even a board with only a few members will find that there are diverse views on a policy or two, a diversity that may not be apparent until the members try to commit the policy to writing. In general, the greater the diversity of views, the greater the cost (time to craft a consensus policy) of the BPM, but also the greater the value (clarity among board members). This axiom holds with boards large and small. Accordingly, we suggest that, rather than assuming that policies are shared across the board, test the notion by following a roadmap that has a large scale, i.e., covers a big area. You may be surprised to learn about differences in perspectives among board members and even between the board and the CEO. Further, the exercise will probably prompt new questions about how the board is governing. You can always stop when you are at the point of diminishing returns, and you will still have a functioning BPM.

"The CEO Doesn't Need or Want More Clarity as to the Board's Policies"

It is also not unusual for CEOs to question the benefits of the BPM, which they or their staffs may see as limiting their authority or cramping their style. Some CEOs may prefer to ask forgiveness after the fact rather than to seek permission before the fact. They may think, "If nobody says anything, fine. If I get in trouble with the board, well, I won't do it again." Other CEOs, who may not enjoy the full support of the board, may see the BPM as a ploy to look over their shoulders. Still other CEOs, who feel that they are in competition with the board, may view the BPM as a power play on the part of the board. Even those CEOs who enjoy a strong and trusting relationship with their boards may not want to test that relationship or risk their independence by laboring through a policy-writing exercise.

Most boards we have worked with are sensitive to their relationship with the CEO, and appropriately so. Good CEOs usually know how to build and lead healthy organizations, and boards want to give them the space they need in order to operate. Boards rightly worry about micromanaging their CEOs or burdening them with unnecessary rules or reports. The reaction we often receive from boards is that the BPM is not something that they want to drop on the CEO and risk harm to the relationship or, worse, cause the CEO to resign.

Our Response

We don't minimize the importance of the relationship between the CEO and the board. Indeed, we know of nothing that is more important to the strength of the governance function. But far from jeopardizing the CEO–board relationship, a BPM that is developed by following the roadmap in this book will improve it. Take, for example, the following scenarios:

- *The strong and capable CEO whom the board does not want to risk losing by suggesting that he needs written limitations on his actions.* In such a case, the board may choose to keep the BPM at a high level, giving more attention to board structure and process than to executive parameters (limitations). By working in a collaborative fashion with the CEO, the board can demonstrate how the BPM will make the board a more effective body for the CEO to work with. Good CEOs will see the value of this kind of clarity, since having a properly structured and oriented board makes it far easier for them to manage upward. They don't have to guess at the boundaries, and they needn't wonder about when they are within the board's policy framework. If a BPM is developed using a collaborative process that involves the CEO, the board, and selected members of the staff, the result will be a document that can be understood from the different perspectives and can be seen as a product of constructive communication. Finally, we frequently find strong CEOs who want their boards to set some parameters around certain areas where they feel vulnerable or less able to fend off strong external pressures.

- *The strong, independent CEO who doesn't want to manage upward because she doesn't want a boss.* Such CEOs may be strong, but they are rarely desirable. The board, after all, has the fiduciary and legal responsibility to its stakeholders and to the government. It should be extremely cautious about hiring a CEO who wants a completely free hand in running the organization.

- *A micromanaging board that is constantly involved in the CEO's business, nit-picking here and criticizing there without having a clear delineation of the board's responsibilities and the CEO's duties.* The CEO in this case should welcome an opportunity to sit down with the board, draw clear lines of authority and responsibility, and lay out the expectations of the board against which the CEO will be evaluated. In many cases, the board simply needs to be reminded of its role and the CEO's role. In some cases, the board may be operating at an inappropriately low level because past CEOs were weak. The board may have stepped in and developed an operational rather than a strategic mentality. If the board lacks confidence in the CEO, following the roadmap to the BPM will highlight any board–CEO differences that may exist and deal with them in a straightforward and effective manner.

    In summary, CEOs deserve to know what is expected of them, regardless of whether they are new or veteran, strong or weak, or popular or unpopular. Similarly, boards need a basis on which to evaluate the CEO. The BPM provides a clear channel of communication between the CEO and the board in the critical area of goals and strategies that are shared by the CEO and board. These shared goals and strategies are the foundation for expectations of the CEO, and her evaluation is derived logically from these expectations.

- *Finally there is the matter of the new CEO or a candidate for the CEO position.* How can he know what his relationship with the board will be? The answer is clearly stated within the BPM, where the board's role, structure, and style are described, as are the board–CEO relationship and the parameters that the board has put around the CEO's areas of responsibility. We know of no better document to communicate these key points to a new CEO or CEO candidate.

"Because We Are Required to Keep Minutes of Our Meetings, a BPM Is Redundant"

Some boards take considerable care with their minutes and are diligent in documenting board resolutions. They make sure that the language is agreed upon by the entire board and carefully recorded in the minutes. Boards that are thorough with their minutes normally have good filing systems that facilitate access to resolutions and policy formulation. They reason that pulling these policies into a single document would have only a modest value, which would be exceeded by the cost in time. Moreover, the board would still continue to keep careful minutes and would probably rely on them rather than on the BPM.

Our Response

Most board minutes are written in a general, narrative fashion. Even though they are typically required by law, meeting minutes are rarely written with the kind of specificity needed for well-constructed policies. Rather than articulate policies, minutes tend to document board actions and to reflect ad hoc, time-specific decisions. Archives of minutes are usually very inefficient libraries, and using them to research policies is often clumsy, inaccurate, and time-consuming.

A board that is careful about its minutes, both in substance and in process, will certainly have an easier time researching the minutes archives to determine past and existing policies. Even in these cases, however, the board loses the clear value of the BPM as the single voice of the board, a concept that encompasses not just plain vanilla policies and board resolutions, but also the strategic direction of the organization, board style and structure, and the board–CEO relationship. In addition, assume that you are an incoming board member and you have a choice as to how you become oriented to your new job. Which of these scenarios are you likely to prefer?

> *Scenario 1.* Review several documents, including (1) statements on vision, mission, values, strategy, and current goals, (2) minutes of board meetings from the past five (or more) years, (3) a description of the board, including officers, committees, protocols, periodic reports, and the expectations of board members, and (4) possibly a list of policies, which may or not be in the minutes that you reviewed in (2).
>
> *Scenario 2.* Read the BPM, which covers all of the material in Scenario 1.

Scenario 2 is a decidedly more efficient path for orienting a new board member. The same lopsided comparison applies to anyone who wants to learn about the organization—outside auditors, rating or accreditation units, potential donors, or other interested stakeholders in the organization. The BPM rarely includes information of a confidential nature or for board members' "eyes only," and boards with transparency as one of their values have found the BPM to be particularly effective in reinforcing that value. This is especially true with associations or other member-based nonprofits where the board wants to maintain clear lines of communication with the members.

"It's Too Much Work/Time/Money"

There is work involved in developing a BPM, and most nonprofit board members have a limited amount of time to do the basic necessities of their job. Taking on the major project of writing a manual that they consider to be of dubious value is not high on the list of most boards that we have worked with. There are officers to elect and budgets to pass and funds to solicit and other critical tasks that should not be sacrificed just so that the board can say that it has a policy manual. Nonprofit board members may concede that there are benefits to the BPM, but they feel that they don't have the dollars or the hours to support the effort of developing even a high-level BPM.

Our Response

Developing a BPM is not a trivial exercise, and we do not want to suggest otherwise. The real question, however, is not whether developing a BPM takes work, but whether it takes "too much work." One way to interpret that statement is to ask whether the investment in time and dollars exceeds the benefits that can be expected from a BPM. To that point, we can offer only our observation that for those nonprofits that have followed the roadmap in this book, we have never seen the benefits of developing a BPM fail to exceed the cost—by a substantial margin. Following the roadmap dramatically reduces the cost of developing the BPM without any reduction in the benefits that will accrue.

Admittedly, the measures of these benefits are often subjective and not easy to quantify. In addition, it is difficult to measure a board's reputation with its CEO, the staff, the donors, and other key stakeholders; however, the value of an efficient board with a strong reputation can hardly be minimized. For example, Jim Collins speaks of the flywheel effect of a solid brand or reputation, and he believes that the concept of a flywheel can be applied to a nonprofit as well as to a for-profit organization.[1] We have seen the impact of an integrated BPM on a board, and we believe that it speaks to the quality of the leadership in an organization, which is certainly one of the key components of its reputation. Where flywheels are concerned, your BPM can certainly increase your RPM.

Another way to interpret the statement, "It's too much work," is that developing the BPM will rob the board of time needed for more important basic duties. To that point, we say with confidence that once the BPM is a material part of your governance model, your board will achieve an efficiency that will allow it to more than recoup the time invested in developing the BPM. We find that many board members are frustrated with the amount of time that they need to devote to routine duties. They complain that the content of their meetings is uninspiring and that the talent that resides on the board is underutilized. Integrating the BPM into the governance process not only will allow routine duties to be handled more efficiently, but will help the board proactively identify and prioritize issues for its consideration.

The objective of documenting policy in the BPM is not to avoid the cost in time of discussing different points of view and resolving them with compromise language. On the contrary, there is a sense in which the longer it takes to resolve differences, the greater the need for the resulting policy to be documented. With some boards, there seems to be an attitude that time is saved if controversial topics are deferred or left unaddressed altogether. But leaving fundamental issues unresolved only increases the time that will be needed to discuss and resolve associated issues. Avoiding the tough issues also does a poor job of modeling basic values like integrity, respect, and transparency. Good boards take on issues where there are differences among their members and document the consensus in the BPM. They incur the cost of working out the differences, but they incur them only once. And they recoup those costs when they build on the agreed-upon language in the policy.

A final thought on the "too much time" argument. If you are unconvinced as to the benefit/cost ratio of developing the BPM, you may want to jump to Chapter 12, where we present four case studies of organizations that have embraced the BPM. In each of these cases, although it is difficult to know exactly the total number of person-hours invested before a first draft was taken to the board for approval, we estimate that the average is in the range of twenty-five to forty hours, i.e., the combined time of two or three well-versed board or staff members. Each of the organizations in the case study (Chapter 12) started with our template (see Appendix A), which saved the organizations considerable time over starting from scratch.

"Many of Our Board Documents Just Gather Dust Anyway"

Articles of incorporation and bylaws are not particularly well-thumbed documents. They are drawn up when the organization is founded, normally by an attorney, and they are often considered the territory of the corporate counsel. They are rarely referred to as the board conducts its business, and the majority of the board members are unfamiliar with their contents. Adding another board document to the articles and the bylaws would only increase the number of documents that require an attorney to interpret and that aren't read anyway.

Our Response

We certainly agree that if you develop a BPM and then let it gather dust, you are wasting your time. That's why a necessary part of the roadmap is the third leg, the integration of the BPM into your governance structure. We don't deny that the articles of incorporation get almost no attention and that the bylaws are often written in legal language and infrequently cited. But the BPM should be written in clear, uncomplicated language, and it is always a work in process. Boards that are attentive to their governance duties are constantly adding to, deleting, and modifying their strategies, current goals, and policies. Although the BPM is written in succinct language, we do not recommend that it be written in "legalese." Nor do we recommend that its drafting be delegated to the general counsel or an outside counsel. The BPM is the voice of the entire board, and therefore board members should be highly conversant with what it says and comfortable in drafting its contents.

"We Did One of Those Policy Manuals Once, but We Never Used It"

This is the classic "been there, done that" response. John Carver's Policy Governance model has been around for close to fifteen years, and many nonprofits have attempted to implement it. But, in Carver's own words, "The Policy Governance® model introduced a new and demanding level of excellence to boards and directors. Because it is demanding, . . . it is not for everybody."[2] Some boards have developed a policy manual as described in the Policy Governance model or even a policy manual similar to the

BPM and have not used it to govern their organizations. These boards point to their out-of-date manual and indicate that they have little desire to try the whole policy manual thing again.

Our Response

This may be the toughest reason to respond to, because it seems to cite firsthand experience. Indeed, we have heard from boards that they have "done the policy manual." Unfortunately for the discussion, we believe that they are not comparing apples with apples when they compare the policy manual that they have developed with the BPM that stands at the heart of the roadmap. The BPM that we espouse is never "done." Rather, it is always "doing." Accordingly, we would challenge the rationale that we've "been there, done that." Writing a static BPM is treating it as just another document and not accepting the concept of integrating it as a fundamental element in a governance model. If you don't keep your BPM current, you are not following the roadmap. And if you don't have the board buy-in up front and the commitment to center your governance model on the BPM after it is developed, we recommend that you forgo the process altogether.

✧

In our view, these roadblocks, well-intentioned as they may be, are not reasons to abandon your journey to good governance. In Chapter 5, we describe a process for developing the BPM that has worked for countless nonprofits. In Chapters 6 through 10, we provide detail that informs the thinking of those people involved in the early drafting process. As mentioned earlier, our experience gives us confidence that a knowledgeable staff member or board member can sit down with our template (Appendix A) and the coaching in Chapters 6 through 10 and produce a credible working draft of the BPM in less than two or three workdays. With that order of magnitude level of investment, you can be well on your way to having a functional BPM. If you and your board are ready to "just do it," Chapter 5 will explain how.

The BPM Development Process

We come now to the heart of the roadmap—the development of the BPM. Most of the rest of the book is centered on this process and on moving from the BPM concept to the BPM reality. This chapter outlines the process, describes the individual steps, and includes advice for those involved with the drafting and reviewing of the first version of the BPM. As in Chapter 3, where we describe how to present the BPM concept to the board, in this chapter we tend toward a somewhat formal approach to developing the BPM. You may not need the formality suggested in our process, but don't dash into development with the idea that, since you have the commitment of the board, you can rush the BPM to press. Such an approach (1) risks getting a lower-quality, narrowly supported first version of the BPM and (2) forgoes the benefits of learning best practices in governance during the development effort.

The second of these points deserves emphasis. You will see in this chapter that there is work ahead for both the key players in the process and the rest of the board members, but the time that everyone spends on this exercise will be substantially rewarded. Having a workable, widely supported BPM emerge from the drafting process is perhaps reward enough, but with thoughtful engagement of the board in the development process, you will have more than just a BPM at the end. You will have a board that is familiar with best practices in governance and better prepared to ensure that the BPM remains the centerpiece of your governance activities.

Although there are various ways to complete this leg of the journey, we describe here the steps in the process that we have most frequently seen used. For example, Chapter 12 includes four case studies of organizations that have developed BPMs. Each of these organizations basically used the approach laid out in this chapter with only minor variations, and all of them now have fully operating BPMs as an integral part of their governance model. Although the time frame for completing the steps for these organizations ranged from a few weeks to over a year, the differences stemmed largely from differences in the timing between board meetings and from differences in the complexity of the organizations.

Eight Steps to Developing a BPM

The steps in our recommended BPM development process are:

1. Assign a coordinator.
2. Start with a template.
3. Fill in the template with known data.
4. Distribute the draft BPM to a review team.
5. Update and refine the BPM based on review team feedback.
6. Conduct a legal review of the revised BPM.
7. Present the BPM draft to the full board.
8. Begin operating with the approved BPM.

In addition to describing what is involved in each step, we give you an estimate of the time that should be set aside for each step. As implied earlier, however, the times will vary as a result of a number of factors and should be taken as estimates.

Step 1: Assign a Coordinator

This is the person who can move the BPM though its phases and have it emerge as a living, breathing document. We don't call this person the "writer" of the BPM, because we want the board members to think of themselves as the writers. The coordinator essentially facilitates the involvement of the board members and keeps the process moving. The desirable traits of the coordinator include being someone who:

1. Has credibility in the organization and with the board
2. Is productive, objective, and persistent
3. Is also patient and diplomatic
4. Knows well how the organization functions

Some boards look to their general counsel or to an in-house or outside attorney to be the coordinator. While we are not against this approach, be careful to ensure that the BPM is written in straightforward language and not in "legalese." Although we clearly recommend a legal review of the draft BPM (Step 6), we don't want it to be perceived as a document that requires a lawyer to draft or heavily edit.

Other boards will ask a consultant to serve as coordinator. This can be a cost-effective approach if the consultant is familiar with the BPM and is prepared to serve in a coordinator role. A word of caution here as well: For the same reason that you don't want the BPM to be considered the "general counsel's document," you don't want it to be perceived as some "consultant's thing." Skilled consultants will understand the need for ownership across the board and will be able to facilitate the process—especially if they appreciate the board's commitment to the roadmap.

Prior to moving on to Step 2, the coordinator should be prepared to spend a few hours familiarizing himself with the BPM development process, the template that we are recommending in Step 2, and the documents that he will draw from in fleshing out the BPM. Accordingly, we see no more than two or three hours being required for Step 1.

Step 2: Start with a Template

Unless you have a good reason to adopt an organization of your BPM different from those of countless other successful organizations, go with a proven format. The one we offer here consists of five parts, as discussed in Chapter 2:

- Part 1: Introduction and Administration
- Part 2: Organization Essentials
- Part 3: Board Structure and Process
- Part 4: Board–CEO/Staff Relationship
- Part 5: Executive Parameters

It is likely that the board will have selected a format when it made its decision to support the BPM concept and commit to following the roadmap. Therefore, we don't see this step requiring much time from the coordinator. For the remainder of this chapter and the book, we assume that the BPM will be in a format similar to the template in Appendix A.

Step 3: Fill In the Template with Known Data

As your coordinator reads through the template, he will be able to drop in data that are specific to your board, e.g., the organization's vision, its mission, and perhaps its values. The coordinator may also know of existing policies involving other sections, such as the description of existing board committees, the nomination process, and financial controls. With regard to some of the general language associated with the BPM (e.g., the structure and processes of the board, the responsibilities of the board and the officers, and the description of the role and relationship of the CEO), we suggest that the coordinator include the language that is already in the template unless it clearly conflicts with existing policies. Most of the language is standard, and leaving it in the initial draft will allow the board members who review the draft to read it in context and then decide whether to keep it. On policy that is not covered in the template, the coordinator can suggest some language or simply leave the section blank and bring it to the attention of the chair of the committee responsible for the relevant section.

This step can take several hours, depending on the volume of material that the coordinator must go through to pick out policies for insertion into the initial draft. A consultant who is familiar with the BPM template and the development process can usually complete this step in six to eight hours. For purposes of estimating, however, and assuming that you have not hired a consultant, plan on between ten and twelve hours for Step 3.

Step 4: Distribute the Draft BPM to a Review Team

The purpose of the review team is to give the coordinator feedback on the initial draft, to offer other material for the first version of the BPM, and to work with the coordinator to ready the draft for presentation to the board. On the one hand, you will want this group to be small enough to be efficient and manageable. On the other hand, you will want the team to include multiple perspectives and disciplines to provide the coordinator with constructive input and editing. Most boards will include the CEO, the chair, or both among the reviewers. We also recommend that you include on the review team the standing committee chairs or at least one member from each standing committee, as you will want the initial draft to benefit from these different perspectives. As far as it is possible here, select reviewers based on their availability and their willingness to respond to at least one and sometimes several iterations of the draft of the BPM that will initially go to the board. It's better, for example, to have an active, responsive member of a standing committee on the review team than to have the committee chair, who may not have the time to give her input.

In addition to sending this first draft to a review team, you may want to send a copy to each member of the board. Distributing the draft to the entire board may seem premature. After all, you don't need or even want the board to approve this initial draft. Nor do you want the unfinished nature of the draft to lower the members' confidence in the BPM concept. The offsetting benefit to that risk, however, is that the board members will see the BPM from two important perspectives. First, they will see the BPM in its entirety and not simply as isolated sections or parts, giving them a sense of what the final product will look like. Second, as they see the BPM modified and amended, they will appreciate that it starts as and will always be a work in progress. Finally, there is no rule that says that only members of the review team should be heard from during this step, and some other board members may offer useful feedback during the initial draft stage.

The time required of the coordinator for this step is combined with that required for Step 5 because of the give and take of working with the review team. Our estimated level of effort for Steps 4 and 5 is included at the end of the discussion of Step 5.

Step 5: Update and Refine the BPM Based on Review Team Feedback

This step in the process is where your coordinator will earn his spurs, as he is the person you will rely on to encourage the reviewers to read the drafts, give their opinions on certain policies that have been incorporated in the drafts, and identify other policies that should be included. Getting feedback from the reviewers can be done in a committee setting, via e-mail, or one-on-one. The coordinator may need to employ one or all of these techniques to ensure that he gains consensus on the policies in the initial draft of the BPM.

The coordinator needs to be a combination of manager and diplomat as he incorporates the comments from the reviewers. Although he is not the decision maker on drafting policy, he must guide the process so that the various parts and sections are alike in style and level of detail. We have found that in this step, there is a tendency on the part of reviewers to include language that is unnecessarily long and detailed. Coordinators may need to work closely with the reviewers to articulate only the board-level policies that apply. For example, many organizations have financial policies that apply to the day-to-day accounting as well as to board-level parameters. Committee chairs may instinctively try to include too many details in the BPM without distinguishing which are board policy and which are management's operating procedures. Here's where the coordinator can serve as coach to the reviewers, reminding them that the BPM is limited to board policy.

This process of determining which of the existing policies deserve to be in the BPM is a useful training exercise for the review-ers. At the end of the day, however, how deeply the board dips into management prerogatives with its policies is a decision that is fundamental to its role of governing. This step and Step 7, where the full board is involved to confirm the language in the BPM, are like calisthenics for the board members in that they are exercising their ability to make policy at the appropriate level—a level that we have heard described as being somewhere between monitoring and meddling.

The time needed to complete this step and Step 4 varies widely with the size, age, and complexity of the organization; the compe-tence of the coordinator; and the cooperation of the reviewers. Although the calendar time for this step may be weeks and even months because of scheduling conflicts, the actual number of hours put in by the coordinator for these two steps is normally as little as five hours and is rarely more than fifteen hours.

Step 6: Conduct a Legal Review of the Revised BPM

This may be done by your general counsel or by an outside attor-ney. The legal review should consider all areas in which the BPM must conform to other documents, e.g., the articles of incorpora-tion and the bylaws of the organization, as well as any federal or state laws that might be relevant. It is a good idea to ensure that the attorney who conducts the review is well acquainted with the BPM, its role in the hierarchy of documents, and its role in the governance structure. Otherwise, you might see a tendency for your attorney to cover all legal and even political bases in the BPM. We mentioned that there is no requirement or even prefer-ence that the coordinator be an attorney. If he is, however, we still recommend an independent legal review. Finally, in response to the legal review, while you want to be careful to heed the advice of your attorney, keep the BPM clear and readable. The BPM is the voice of the board, not a contract that is designed to protect your board against every legal challenge.

This step requires very little time from the coordinator, unless there are substantial comments from the legal review that have to be worked into the BPM. Normally, the calendar time for the legal review is a week or two, but the actual time needed from the coordinator is only three hours or less. Because we are not attorneys, we are reluctant to give an estimate of the amount of time required for the legal review, but we believe that a lawyer who has been properly briefed on the BPM can complete it in a few hours.

Step 7: Present the BPM Draft to the Full Board

When you are preparing to present the first version of the BPM to the board, don't let perfection stand in the way of progress. Not even the revised draft will be 100 percent complete and acceptable to everyone on the board. Don't wait until there is a critical mass of policies in the BPM before adopting it and making it operational. There will be plenty of sections that are either to be written or to be agreed upon. If there are sections where the board is not comfortable with the policies or the language, leave them out. Even a BPM that is essentially just the initial boilerplate language can serve its role, and you can wait for the substance (board policies and decisions) to evolve.

There will be preparation time required of the coordinator and possibly some follow-up time, depending on how many additions or modifications the board identifies. Most of the preparation involves distributing copies of the draft to the board members and ensuring that they have any supplemental material that may be helpful during the meeting where the draft is discussed. The estimated time needed from the coordinator, therefore, is less than three hours.

Step 8: Begin Operating with the Approved BPM

The coordinator can now hand off his duties to the secretary or whoever the BPM says will maintain it (BPM Part 1, Section 1.7 in the template). The coordinator will have put in somewhere between twenty and twenty-five hours, the reviewers perhaps another three to five hours, and each of the other board members two to three hours. The product of this input is a BPM that is operational and a board that:

1. Comprises committees that translate their recommendations into language that will go into the BPM.
2. Uses the BPM to orient and train new members.
3. Has a CEO who asks for clarification on the issues in the form of policy guidance and who assists the board in drafting new policies.
4. Is equipped to carry out its governance functions using the best practices in the nonprofit world.

In short, the BPM will begin doing its job by helping the board members and the CEO do their jobs.

CHAPTER 6

BPM Part 1: Introduction and Administration

This and the next four chapters are intended to guide you in fairly explicit terms through the development of a BPM for your board. We will "walk you through" the full BPM template in Appendix A, addressing each of the five parts in order. As we explain each section of the template and give tips for writing that section, we copy the relevant text from Appendix A (using shaded text) to avoid your having to flip back and forth between this material and Appendix A.

Our template is designed to suggest both form and substance. We want to show you what has worked for countless nonprofits from the standpoint of the organization of their board policies as well as from the standpoint of the content of those policies. However, we are constantly editing our own template in minor ways as we learn from others. So please tailor the language of the policies to your board and organize them as you see fit. We will give you the rationale for both the content and the placement of policies, but we have seen other variations of the BPM that work well for the organizations that designed them.

Where to Place Part 1

Part 1 is rarely more than two pages long and serves mainly to alert the first-time reader to the purpose and format of the BPM as well as its care and feeding by the board. Some organizations that we have worked with see Part 1 as a cover sheet that accompanies the BPM for the first-time reader. Because they see the text of Part 1 as rarely changing and as articulating administrative procedures rather than board policies, they prefer to put this material either in a transmittal memo or in an addendum to the BPM.

We don't agree with that approach, even though we acknowledge that Part 1 requires few changes after its initial draft and that it is concerned mainly with the rationale for the BPM and how it will be maintained. We believe that putting the Introduction and Administration section up front in the BPM not only educates the first-time reader, but also serves as a friendly reminder to veterans of the BPM of its purpose and the process by which it is maintained. Let's start with a suggested main title and status sentence.

Working Through Part 1

With reference to the template in Appendix A, starting at the title:

> Board Policies Manual (BPM) for ABC, Inc.
>
> *Note:* This version of the BPM was approved by the board on January 21, 2007, and reflects several changes from the previous version, which should be discarded.

We suggest that you choose a main heading and stick with it. The BPM will become like a household name after several reviews. The status note is very important because a board that meets, say, three times a year is likely to see six versions of the BPM during the course of the year—one version prior to each meeting (which includes recommendations for changes) and another version following each meeting (which shows the results of board decisions during that meeting). The footers on each page should also clearly identify which version this is, e.g., "ABC, Inc. BPM—Proposed Changes for March 10, 2007, Board Meeting—Page 1 of 14."

Part 1: Introduction and Administration

This Board Policies Manual (BPM) contains all of the current standing (ongoing) policies adopted by the board of [ORGANIZATION] since the initial approval of the BPM on [INITIAL APPROVAL DATE].

1.1 **Reasons for Adoption.** The reasons for adopting this BPM include:

- Efficiency of having all ongoing board policies in one place
- Ability to quickly orient new board members to current policies
- Elimination of redundant or conflicting policies over time
- Ease of reviewing current policy when considering new issues
- Providing clear, proactive policies to guide the chief executive officer (CEO) and staff
- Modeling an approach to governance that other organizations might use

Section 1.1 efficiently conveys to the reader what the BPM contains and why it has been developed. Until the board and the staff members understand and embrace this information, the power of the living document is not appreciated. As much as we would like to see it, the BPM does not enjoy widespread name recognition the way, for example, the bylaws do. If it did, we wouldn't need to explain what it contains or why it is useful.

The lead sentence also contains the date of the original acceptance of the BPM, which signals when the shift from archives of minutes and ad hoc policies to this governance management system of putting all ongoing (standing, some call them) policies in one document took place.

1.2 Consistency. Each policy in this document is expected to be consistent with the law, the articles of incorporation, and the bylaws, all of which have precedence over these board policies. Except for time-limited or procedural-only board decisions (approving minutes, electing an officer, etc.), which are recorded in regular board minutes, all standing policies shall be included or referred to in this document. The CEO is responsible for developing organizational and administrative policies and procedures that are consistent with this BPM.

This section restates the principles reflected in Figure 2-2, "Hierarchy of Organizational Policies"; clarifies which policies are included in the BPM; and includes the requirement that any policies and procedures that the CEO may develop for her staff and her organization must be consistent with the BPM. We discussed in Chapter 2 how the BPM fits with such documents as the articles of incorporation and the bylaws and how all other organizational policies must conform with the BPM. The exception for time-limited and procedure-only decisions is inserted here to make it clear that routine board actions such as approving the minutes, approving a transaction, electing an officer, and so on are material for the meeting minutes, but not for the BPM. Refer again to Figure 2-3, which summarizes the difference between what we consider board "decisions" and board "policies."

1.3 Transition. Whether adopted part by part or as a complete document, as soon as some version of the BPM is voted on as the "one voice" of the board, those policies are deemed to supersede any past policy that might be found in old minutes unless a prior board resolution or contract obligates the organization with regard to a specific matter. If any actual or apparent conflict arises between the BPM and other policies or board resolutions, the matter shall be resolved by the chair or by the entire board as may be appropriate.

This section restates a fundamental principle of the BPM: that it is the one voice of the board. If something is not in the BPM, it's not a policy of the board. For boards that are just getting started with their BPM, this sentence may not be appropriate yet. But at the point when the board approves even a partial BPM, the board needs to tell the world (including any judge), "Hey, if you see an inconsistency between the policies in this BPM and some policy adopted by the board fifteen years ago, this BPM supersedes that old policy."

1.4 Changes. These policies are meant to be reviewed constantly and are frequently reviewed and refined. The CEO helps the board formulate new language in the BPM by distributing proposed changes in advance. When language is recommended for deletion, it is shown in ~~strikethrough~~ format. Proposed new language is <u>underlined</u>. Each section with a proposed change can be preceded by the # sign to help readers quickly locate proposed changes. Any change to this BPM must be approved by the full board. Proposed changes may be submitted by any board member as well as by the CEO. In most cases, proposed changes shall be referred to and reviewed by the appropriate committee before being presented to the board for action. Whenever changes are adopted, a new document should be printed, dated, and quickly made available to the board and staff. The previous version should be kept on a disk for future reference if needed.

Like most sections in Part 1, this section is self-explanatory. Although it is administrative in nature, it communicates a couple of important principles for keeping the BPM current. One principle is that policies need not always emanate from the board. In our experience, the CEO proposes most of the changes in the BPM. That's natural, because a large portion of the BPM consists of policies that the staff has to live with every day. Remember that either the CEO or board members can formulate and propose board policy, but only the full board can decide what actually is board policy. Bob recalls that in his last CEO role, he proposed an average of ten to twelve BPM changes (some minor tweaks; some major shifts in policy) prior to every meeting. When a board committee reviews the CEO's suggested changes that fall in the sections assigned to it, the committee will usually either agree with the CEO and recommend a change, flatly disagree and not recommend a change, or modify the CEO's suggestion and recommend new language. Making BPM improvements is a partnership between the CEO and the board. Figure 6-1 summarizes the roles of the board and the CEO with respect to the various actions involved in developing policies.

Another principle is keeping the BPM up to date. This is usually a thirty-minute task following each board meeting, and it should be done by someone who has kept good notes. A tip: Board minutes do not need to repeat every motion to change the BPM, but can simply state that the board, following committee recommendations and discussion, adopted changes to the BPM (see attached updated BPM).

Also in the template are instructions on how changes are presented on paper and eventually incorporated. There are any number of ways to highlight changes with modern word-processing software, and we are not wedded to any one approach. We do, however, suggest including whatever technique is chosen in the BPM to facilitate the review of proposed changes so that everyone can quickly focus on the proposed changes throughout the BPM.

FIGURE 6-1. Board vs. CEO/Staff Roles in Policy Development.

BOARD POLICY	BOARD	CEO/STAFF
FORMULATION Identify needs, then formulate and consider options	YES	YES
DETERMINATION Legal responsibility to decide	YES	NO
IMPLEMENTATION CEO's job—If directors help, it's as a volunteer	NO	YES
MONITORING* Formal judgment of results based on reports from staff	YES	NO

*The most neglected of these roles in most organizations is the board's responsibility to monitor results, i.e., determining whenever they set a major goal what data will be needed by them to determine how well it is being achieved. The kind of data the board wants, and when, is normally included in the BPM.

1.5 Specificity. Each new policy will be drafted to fit in the appropriate place within the BPM. Conceptually, policies should be drafted from the "outside in," i.e., the broadest policy statement should be presented first, then the next broadest, etc., down to the level of detail that the board finds appropriate for board action and below which management is afforded discretion as to how it implements the policies in this BPM.

This section alerts the reader as to how the BPM is organized. Writing policies in the BPM from the "outside in" is a standard outlining structure, e.g., Section 2.1 is a broad or high-level policy, and Sections 2.1.1, 2.1.2, and so on are more detailed policies that support Section 2.1. Your organization may prefer a different method of outlining, for example, using letter designations. You may even choose to label the parts and sections of the BPM differently. We are not wedded to a specific format, but be sure that your format accommodates the "outside-in" approach.

The principle that is highlighted in this section is that the board decides how much guidance or discretion to give to the CEO and then drafts its policies to a level that reflects that guidance. The CEO therefore understands that she is permitted to work within the boundaries established in the BPM.

1.6 Oversight Responsibility. Below are the parts, the committees primarily responsible for drafting and reviewing those parts, and the individuals given authority to interpret and make decisions within the scope of those policies:

Part/Section	Oversight Committee	Implementation Authority
1. Introduction	Governance Committee	CEO
2. Organization Essentials	Full Board	CEO
3. Board Structure and Processes	Governance Committee	Board Chair
4. Board–CEO/Staff Relationship	Executive Committee	Chair/CEO
5. Executive Parameters		
5.1 General Guidance	Government Committee	CEO
5.2 Finance	Finance Committee	CEO
5.3 Programs	Program Committee	CEO
5.4 Advancement	Advancement Committee	CEO
5.5 Audit and Compliance	Audit and Compliance Committee	CEO
5.6 Miscellaneous	As appropriate	CEO

The BPM is a book that is approved only by the board, not a document that is maintained by a select person or group. That said, we like to see some organization of that corporate responsibility. This section identifies which committee will take the lead on a particular part of the BPM and which individual is given the authority to implement the policies in that part. Note that the words are "primarily responsible for drafting and reviewing those parts." There are no restrictions on who may propose modifications to the BPM—or draft the specific language, for that matter.

> **1.7 Maintenance of Policies.** The secretary shall ensure that staff members record and publish all standing policies correctly. The CEO or the CEO's designee shall maintain the policies file and provide updated copies to the board whenever the policies change, or upon request. The board will ask that legal counsel review this BPM biennially to ensure compliance with the law. Discrete documents referred to in the BPM will be kept in a three-ring notebook called the Board Reference Book.

If your board has truly integrated the BPM into its governance process, there will be frequent changes. Every change warrants a new BPM, even if the change is minor. An adjustment of a word or two may not seem to justify generating an entire new BPM, but the discipline of incorporating every change, however small, avoids any question about the currency of your BPM. Bob had a rule that he or his staff would never even correct a misspelling in the board's BPM, waiting until he proposed BPM changes prior to the next meeting. The board might laugh at such minor recommendations, but this approach taught both board and staff that "every word" in the BPM belonged to the board, not to the staff.

In Chapter 3, we discuss the role of the general counsel in both the original drafting of the document and its ongoing maintenance. Although the general counsel or an outside attorney is accustomed to board documents and would have little trouble with either drafting or maintaining the BPM, we have seen too many BPMs become just another legal document that is relegated to an occasional reference or citation and never truly integrated into the governance model. Still, the general counsel has an important role in keeping the BPM consistent with the articles of incorporation and the bylaws, as well as with any statutes or government policies that may apply. In the template, we suggest that biennial reviews of the BPM by legal counsel are sufficient. With any questionable proposed policy, legal counsel might be asked for comment prior to the policy's adoption and incorporation into the BPM.

The Board Reference Book (BRB) is a supplement to the BPM; we discuss it in Chapter 11 and you can download a more detailed description of the BRB. We recommend maintaining a reference book of relevant documents that are of interest to your board so that the BPM itself remains lean and readable. You will have many board-related documents that are relevant to policies cited in the BPM, but that are also bulky and often written in legal language. Mentioning the Board Reference Book in this section of the BPM simply makes it clear that the board wants these documents maintained separate from the BPM.

Your board members may seldom change Part 1 of the BPM after it is first written, but the key principles that it contains underlie the third leg of the roadmap (integration of the BPM). Even though Part 1 receives the fewest changes, they are policies relating to the BPM itself and, we believe, need to be in the BPM as reminders for both board and staff.

CHAPTER 7

BPM Part 2: Organizational Essentials

One of the principal roles of the board is to provide strategic direction to the organization. Why do we exist? What are the outcomes we expect? Which values should guide everything we do? Some boards are heavily involved with strategic planning. Other boards tend to leave the strategy up to the CEO and simply measure the progress of the organization against the strategic plan. But regardless of how active the board is in the actual planning process, it must own the strategy and see to it that the CEO stays focused on its implementation.

Purpose and Content

Some readers may not perceive concepts like the mission, vision, and values of an organization as "policies" and therefore may see them as being out of place in a board policies manual. However, we consider Part 2 of the BPM as a type of compass setting for the organization and the board. Many people consider this the most important of the five parts of the BPM because it focuses everyone in the same direction. This part is the "what and why" of the organization. As such, it is often the most challenging part to write.

We have characterized the BPM as the "one voice" of the board. With that in mind, we view these "organization essentials" as establishing the key themes of the organization early in the document. These essentials give the board an opportunity to underscore the purpose, character, and strategic direction of the organization. These are the reasons that board members agree to serve, staff members agree to work, and donors agree to give.

In his Policy Governance model, John Carver separates board policies into two categories: "ends" and "means." He describes "ends policies" as:

> The board's expectations about (1) the benefit, difference, or outcome in consumers' lives that the organization is to produce, (2) the persons for whom the difference is to be made, . . . and (3) the cost or relative worth of the benefits. . . . Ends [policies] simply answer the questions What good? For which people? At what cost?[1]

We agree that those are the strategic questions: Which benefits? For whom? At what cost (or priority)? The entries in BPM Part 2 are designed to address issues similar to Carver's ends policies. There are, however, some additional features that we like to see in Part 2, namely, a listing of organization values and a summary of both the strategic goals and the tactical (current) goals for the organization. We prefer to see a list of values in this part because they are the primary determinant of an organization's culture. We believe that the board should be involved in setting expectations for the culture of the organization. This is especially true in the nonprofit world, where an organization's success so often turns on its reputation. It is difficult enough to raise money in the philanthropic marketplace even with a strong reputation. Organizations that rely on contributions and that have a questionable reputation, or are unknown, must wrestle especially hard with the topics in BPM Part 2.

Including the strategic goals in Part 2 allows the board to put its stamp on the high-level direction of the organization. Including the tactical goals in Part 2 is, in our view, a good way to (1) tie these goals to the strategic goals and (2) keep them in front of the board members and the CEO. We see these current goals as the primary basis for the CEO's evaluation, and as such, they warrant being frequently exposed to both the evaluator (the board) and the evaluated (CEO). Some CEOs we have worked with use the current goals (Section 2.8 in our template) as the outline for their presentation to the board at every formal meeting. The CEO is saying in effect, "Here are your expectations; here is how I am working to meet them; and here are the results to date." We highly encourage this practice. It keeps the focus of the board in line with the focus of the CEO and allows the board to monitor progress toward key goals on an ongoing basis.

Part 2 of the Template

From this point forward, we hope that you will be stimulated to think of your board and whether the content of our template, shown in shaded text, will work for you at this time.[2] We are wedded neither to these specific sections nor to the exact wording of each one. Some boards have taken our template, shown in full in Appendix A, and used almost every word. Others have used the template mainly as a guide, which they add to and subtract from at will. Feeling free to *adapt* rather than simply *adopt* is important. With that caveat, let's move forward.

2.1 Our vision is . . .

A commonly held definition of a vision statement is that it is a statement about what you want your organization to become. It often will be couched in aspirational terms, such as to be "the most innovative in a certain geographic area," to be "among those listed in a prestigious publication," or to be known as "one of the premier organizations in a particular field."

Another approach to a vision statement is to describe the effect that your organization will have, e.g., "enhance the reputation of the arts in a certain city," "highlight the plight of indigent people in a certain area," or "increase the awareness of a disease for a sector of the population."

A third approach is becoming more popular, and it is one that we tend to favor for nonprofits. It is a statement that envisions a "big outcome" or result or change that you would like to see in the world—a result that your organization will contribute to, but that will need help from sometimes hundreds of other organizations and even governments. For example, a community literacy center might say, "Our vision is that all adults in our city read at the sixth-grade level." That is obviously a goal that needs good work by far more organizations than the literacy center alone, yet it identifies the organization's efforts with those of other organizations wishing to move society closer to accomplishing the vision. Another example is a drug abuse prevention clinic that might have the vision of a "drug-free city," another good outcome that will require help from many other organizations in every sector if it is to be achieved. But it gives everyone—board, staff, beneficiaries, and donors—a high calling to shoot for.

Although an organization can use some license to imagine a better world because of its efforts along with the efforts of other organizations, when it comes to articulating its mission, the board needs to be more specific.

2.2 Our mission is . . .

Whether or not you have a vision statement is not nearly as important as having a clear mission statement. If you already have a mission statement that everyone has reviewed recently and is comfortable with, simply plug it into the template and move on.

If you have not given your mission statement a thorough review recently, maybe this is a good time to do so. Again, different authors tend to define "good" mission statements differently. We like those that define an outcome or result that your organization could conceivably achieve over time. One of our friends likes to say that the mission should be "out of reach but not out of sight." What would your community, your region, or even the world look like if you eventually achieved what you set out to do? "To eradicate poverty in the world" may be a good vision statement, but it's not a mission that could be reached. A more appropriate mission statement might be, "Reduce by 50 percent the number of people in our county living under the federal poverty level." That is specific. We know that some organizations have an easier time stating their mission in measurable terms than others. A college, for example, may struggle with specificity in its mission statement, but it should not be satisfied with something like, "Preparing citizens for leadership in the world." Every college could say that. The question is what distinguishes you from other organizations in the same sector.

We have seen many mission statements that would more appropriately be labeled descriptions of what an organization does. So a statement like "Our mission is to distribute used textbooks to schools in Africa" is helpful, but defining the desired outcome of the organization's work would make a better mission statement.

It is not worth belaboring the discussion of mission statements. The key is that the board and the staff are crystal clear about what they intend to do and why, and that this is affirmed by other major stakeholders. Once the board agrees on the essentials, then staff members can come up with catchy taglines, campaign slogans, radio spots, and so on that are on target and present an integrated brand and proper positioning of your organization.

Finally, a good mission statement should point to specific data to monitor in order to give an organization confidence that it is making progress. Some things are more measurable in quantitative terms than others, while other missions must be measured in qualitative terms, such as through opinion surveys. Thinking through how you will measure success is another aspect of writing a good mission statement.

2.3 The **values** that guide everything we do are . . .

Every organization has a corporate culture, which is determined by the values that are reflected both internally among the staff and externally to its community and the public at large. In the same way that an individual's character is defined by the consistency with which he honors his values privately and publicly, an organization's culture is defined by the consistency between the organization's published values and the actual values that it maintains in all aspects of its operations. Does the organization walk the talk in all of its dealings?

To answer the walk-the-talk question, you must first ask if you have thoughtfully articulated a value set, which is essentially "the talk." Are your values in writing, and have they penetrated your organization? A well-developed value set that is shared at every level of the organization, starting with the board, will create a corporate culture in which good staff members and volunteers want to work and an environment that is conducive to achieving the mission. These values should influence everything that the organization does. In addition, the board, the CEO, and the staff should all be held responsible (read measured) for how well they reflect these values.

Stating the values explicitly in Part 2 sets them alongside the mission, vision, and strategy. The message from the board, therefore, is not simply what the organization does, but how it does it. As with the vision and mission statements, the techniques and formats for listing values vary widely from organization to organization. Usually, the primary values desired by a board can be captured in four, five, or six short phrases or sentences. Remember that values should be honored not for show, but for success.

2.4 The **moral owners** to whom the board feels accountable (e.g., members, alumni, donors, or taxpayers) are . . .

We believe that every board needs to feel accountable to a larger group. Again, we like John Carver's suggestion that, just as for-profit businesses answer to stockholders who have equity shares in the business, nonprofit organizations have "moral owners," and the board should feel accountable to them and should find ways to "link" with them. For a membership organization, the moral owners are usually the same as the primary beneficiaries (see the discussion of Section 2.5). For example, when lawyers pay dues to an association of lawyers, they assume that they and other members will be considered the primary beneficiaries of the association.

Things become more difficult for nonmember associations. Often it is easier to identify the primary beneficiaries (e.g., students or homeless persons or drug-addicted teens), than to identify the moral owners. Here is a clear example of the distinction: students are the primary beneficiaries of an independent private elementary school, but parents and major donors are probably the moral owners with whom the board wants to stay in touch.

If this section brings focus and clarity to your organization, we believe it is worth thinking about. The board links with these moral owners through an annual report, a survey requesting input, an open forum, focus groups, and other such methods. Even if moral owners hear frequently from the chief executive, hearing from members of the board can bring an extra measure of linkage with them.

We have seen some nonprofit boards worry that listing specific groups might result in other interested parties feeling left out. After all, they argue, any nonprofit that is helping anyone is benefiting the entire community and not just a subset of the community. We haven't observed this reaction from "unlisted parties," but our sense is that if a group expresses some concern over not being listed in the BPM, maybe it should be listed after all. Our purpose in this section is to encourage you to identify people and groups that the board will make a conscious attempt to connect with on a continuing basis.

2.5 The primary **beneficiaries** of our services are . . .

Assuming that the board identified its moral owners/stake-holders in Section 2.4, we suggest being explicit about the primary beneficiaries in Section 2.5. This also helps bring important focus to a number of other policies. The key word is *primary*. Often a board thinks that it can serve too many people, resulting in a lack of focus and spreading scarce resources too thin. This section more or less answers the question, "Who are your customers?" You can't be all things to all people. Experienced nonprofits tend to have a defined primary beneficiary group (e.g., seniors in Monroe County or fifteen- to eighteen-year-old girls). The concept of segmentation is important. Because it's clear that senior citizens and teenagers have vastly different motivations, needs, and interests, we encourage you to be specific in defining your primary beneficiaries (Section 2.5). This can be done in a few phrases. And if you find it helpful, go ahead and identify both primary and secondary beneficiary groups, an exercise that by itself will help set priorities for budgets, hiring, and programs.

2.6 The major general **functions** and the approximate percentage of total effort that is expected to be devoted to each are . . .

We like boards that drive down yet another level in guiding the chief executive to accomplish the mission. While a good board will identify the major functions, a great board will find mutual agreement with the chief executive on the priority given to each function, even if it was stated as generally as "Priority A, Priority B, and Priority C." Another way to express the contents of this section might be: "Our primary functions and the approximate amount of program funds allocated to them are training (40 percent), research (20 percent), and Web resources (40 percent)." Whatever level of specificity the board can reach (without getting into management decisions) improves the chances of organizational effectiveness. This is one of many, many areas in which miscommunication can result from differing assumptions. We have seen boards discuss this issue with their top staff members and, independently, write down their assumptions of the relative weightings of their major programmatic functions. One function could get a rating of 10 percent from the staff and 70 percent from the board! The lesson: Pursue clarity and unity wherever possible.

2.7 The primary **strategies** by which we will fulfill our mission include . . .

Often the content of this section is simply an excerpt from the strategic plan. It is included to emphasize the board's involvement in, ownership of, and support for the strategy. There is seldom a need to include detail regarding the strategy. Normally, a quick summary of the strategy or strategies is sufficient, along with a reference to the strategic plan. Examples of different strategy statements might include "leverage a state-of-the-art Web site," "become the primary repository of data on runaway teenagers," "leverage strategic alliances with A and B organizations," or "outsource all functions not essential to accomplishing our mission." Such overall strategies direct the energies of the organization and give the staff members maximum flexibility in how they move in those directions. If the chief executive has not developed a strategic plan, this section simply adds to the building blocks that the board expects to see in the staff's plan.

2.8 The major organizational **goals** and monitoring indicators for the next three years are . . .

This section is where boards differ on the level of specificity that they should address.

Usually this section is drafted by the chief executive because it moves closer to what her staff needs to be doing to fulfill all the policies in Part 2, as well as remain within the parameters in Part 5. Accordingly, this section should be written at a greater level of detail than Section 2.6, on primary functions, and Section 2.7, on primary strategies. Here is where the board and the CEO articulate their partnership for the next twelve to eighteen months by laying out the specific goals (or objectives, if you prefer) that have been mutually agreed upon. These specific goals become the core of what the board will use to evaluate the CEO, along with her more personal goals. And they give the CEO leverage with her senior staff in holding them accountable for goals that are delegated to them.

This section is one that is likely to change at least annually and possibly even more frequently. There is no reason to keep accomplished goals on the list and every reason to add new goals as new opportunities or unexpected surprises require. These goals help inform fund-raising initiatives, staff hires, and staff training, but only if they are current, held by both the board and the CEO, and consistently monitored.

> **2.9 Strategic Plans.** The board is expected to think strategically at all times. The CEO is expected to develop a staff strategic plan based on the policies in this BPM, update it as necessary, link major activities in the plan to the relevant sections of this BPM, and provide copies of the plan to the board for information by April 1 each year.

Although we have worked with boards that have a board strategic planning committee, we prefer that this function not be housed in a board committee. We would rather see the board give the CEO the lead on strategic planning, allowing him to tap individual board members with specific skills and experiences as participants. Any strategic plan worth its salt requires giving time and staff resources to technical and legal issues, budget, fund-raising, staff assignments, and much more. The average board has neither the time nor the necessary information to put such a plan together.

Allowing the CEO to take the lead does not mean that board members are shut out of the planning process. It simply means that board members work under the leadership of the CEO.

We are, of course, not suggesting that the board delegate any portion of its ownership of the strategic plan. Notice how we state the task for the CEO in the template's language. The board is saying that the CEO should write the plan with specific links (references to the BPM) so that the board sees how the ideas in the plan accomplish specific board policies. Notice further that we suggest that the full board review the plan—not approve it, as that would make the strategic plan a board document. We prefer that the strategic operating plan remain in Box 6, "CEO-Level Policies," in Figure 2-2.

But what should a board do if it reads the plan annually and doesn't like certain parts of it? The first question we would ask in this case is whether the plan is consistent with the BPM, i.e., the board's policies, particularly those listed in this part (Part 2). In other words, does the disagreement stem from differences of personal opinion between the board members and the CEO or from the CEO going outside the guidance in BPM Part 2? If the latter, then the board has to make the decision to either modify the policy in the BPM or direct the CEO to bring the plan into line with the BPM. You will hear this principle over and over. Boards are not to micromanage. Allow members of the professional staff to make the decisions that they are most qualified to make. The board should keep flying at 5,000 feet unless the organization is clearly off the course that has been set by mutual agreement of the board and the CEO and stated in the BPM. Only then should a board dip down and redirect the CEO with more detailed policies.

We are often asked about the role of the board in strategic planning and the dynamics of working with the CEO and the staff. When we work with boards and CEOs on strategic planning, we use a summary sheet similar to the one entitled "Overview of a Good Strategic Planning Model for Nonprofit Organizations," which is on the list of downloadable documents in Appendix B and which highlights some of the issues and principles that we emphasize in the strategic planning process. Even if you have a strategic planning approach that you are comfortable with, our overview may suggest some ways to refine your process.

✧

We trust that you appreciate the critical role that Part 2 plays in the communication between the board and the CEO and further appreciate that writing it is not easy. Boards could spend many meetings debating these few pages called Part 2. But it is time spent wisely. A well-crafted set of organization essentials will give you a great start on forming the rest of your BPM. Part 3 focuses on the policies that the board sets for its own structure and process, a much easier part because good practices are emerging that apply to all boards, regardless of what their organization essentials might be.

CHAPTER 8

BPM Part 3: Board Structure and Process

This part of the BPM is fundamentally a statement of what the board says to itself about how it will be structured, how it will operate, and what it expects of its officers and its members. Although an organization's bylaws will normally address the makeup of the board—its size, the terms of its members, how they are elected, and so on—BPM Part 3 adds specificity and clarity to these descriptors. BPM Part 3 also includes language that expresses the style of the board, the culture that is sought, and the expectations of each board member. These statements speak to the governance philosophy that underlies the way the board will carry out its duties. Although they are rarely found in the bylaws, they are valuable points of reference. These qualitative standards of performance touch everything that the board does and basically establish a benchmark of behavior for the board as a unit and for its individual members.

As a reminder of the relationship between the bylaws and the BPM, we refer you again to the hierarchy of documents in Figure 2-2, which shows the relationship of the BPM to the other board documents, such as the articles of incorporation and the bylaws.

As we point out in Chapter 2, the articles of incorporation is a document that the organization submits to the secretary of state to receive approval to operate in that state as a nonprofit corporation, and it provides the basic information needed to establish the organization, including its name, its purpose, and how it will dispose of its assets if it is dissolved. The articles of incorporation also identify the initial board of directors. The bylaws are more detailed, describing how the corporation will function, defining the board and officers' roles and terms of office, providing rules regarding meetings, defining how amendments can be made, and so on.

The articles of incorporation may be changed by the board, but the organization is required to notify the secretary of state of the changes, and it must pay a fee to accompany this filing. The articles are normally written at a very general level to preserve flexibility and minimize the need for amendments. Therefore, they are infrequently read, let alone changed.

The rules governing changes to an organization's bylaws may differ depending on whether it is a member organization (e.g., an association) or a nonmember organization. Boards of nonmember organizations and those of some member organizations may have the authority to amend the bylaws, but these changes may require approval by a supermajority on the board, e.g., two-thirds or three-quarters. For many member organizations, changes in the bylaws must be approved by the members. In these cases, the bylaws include an explanation of what constitutes a member, how members vote, and other rules that apply to the members' involvement in the governance process. Some member organizations will have a hybrid set of rules for changing the bylaws that allow the board to make most changes, but that require a member vote on changes in certain key sections.

Whether or not yours is a member organization, we recommend that you keep your bylaws short and general, especially if you are following the roadmap in this book. Good bylaws usually don't exceed ten to twelve pages. Omitting the detail from the bylaws and leaving it for the BPM has clear benefits, including:

- It reduces the frequency of changes to the bylaws, whose revisions may need to be submitted to the IRS.

- It facilitates changes in policies to respond to the current needs of the organization.
- It allows the BPM to contain in one place all the information normally needed to understand the board's structure and processes.
- It reduces redundancies or the chance of inconsistencies between the BPM and the bylaws.

If your bylaws currently contain detail that you don't believe is necessary in light of the discussion in this chapter, we suggest that you leave them alone for the time being. Once you have an operational BPM, you can always go back and amend the bylaws to reconcile the two documents. This usually means that you will start by reducing some redundancies between the two documents. For example, if your bylaws include some detail on the process for nominating board members, you may choose to describe the complete process in the BPM as well. Bear in mind that the BPM must comply with all the requirements that are in the bylaws. Later on, you may pull the detail out of the bylaws so that it appears in the BPM alone. Throughout this chapter we will touch on how to work with bylaws in developing the BPM.

> *3.1 Governing Style.* The board will approach its task with a style that emphasizes outward vision rather than an internal preoccupation, encouragement of diversity in viewpoints, strategic leadership more than administrative detail, clear distinction of board and staff roles, and proactivity rather than reactivity. In this spirit, the board will:
>
> 3.1.1 Enforce upon itself and its members whatever discipline is needed to govern with excellence. Discipline shall apply to matters such as attendance, respect for clarified roles, speaking to management and the public with one voice, and self-policing of any tendency to stray from the governance structure and processes adopted in these board policies.

3.1.2 Be accountable to its stakeholders and the general public for competent, conscientious, and effective accomplishment of its obligations as a body. It will allow no officer, individual, or committee of the board to usurp this role or hinder this commitment.

3.1.3 Monitor and regularly discuss the board's own processes and performance, seeking to ensure the continuity of its governance functions by selection of capable directors, orientation and training, and evaluation.

3.1.4 Be an initiator of policy, not merely a reactor to staff initiatives. The board, not the staff, will be responsible for board performance.

A governing board is more an expression of "ownership" than an extension of "management." In the nonprofit world, we call those groups *moral owners* or *stakeholders*. Each board has a particular personality, culture, or style. We believe it is important for each board to be proactive in defining its philosophy and style.

When the word *style* is used to describe an individual in our society, it often is intended to encompass a combination of characteristics pertaining to that person—how he looks, the way he communicates, how he dresses, his hobbies, how he makes decisions, and perhaps other individual features. In a business setting, although we use shorthand labels such as authoritarian vs. democratic, inclusive vs. exclusive, decisive vs. indecisive, or humble vs. self-centered to describe a person's style, a single descriptor is rarely sufficient to paint an accurate portrait of this person and the way he conducts himself. We normally need a list of characteristics and personality traits in order to understand who he is and what we can expect from him.

Boards, too, can be said to have a style, which tends to describe how board members operate together. For example, boards often contain members with different personalities and points of view, which can lead to the development of competing factions or cliques. Working as a unit is difficult unless there is agreement on how the board will function. Recognizing that different boards have different habits and cultures, the purpose of BPM Section 3.1 is to establish some principles for the board that will encourage individual thinking, but at the same time emphasize corporate co-operation. In Section 3.1, you want to capture the character and culture of the board. The contents of the section explain how the board wants to describe itself and how it wants to be described by those outside the board. In the end, you and your colleagues on the board want to be seen as a group with character, not as a bunch of characters, and you want those outside your board to like its "style."

The sample language in the template is essentially a set of instructions from the board to itself, and, while these instructions may seem elementary and even unnecessary, they truly set the compass for everything that follows in the remainder of the BPM. To summarize, this section directs the board to:

- Think and act strategically.
- Lead the organization through policies, rather than managing the staff.
- Hold itself accountable to its stakeholders for its performance.
- Hold its members individually accountable for their performance.
- Make decisions as a board and not default to the view of an individual or subgroup.
- Commit to looking outward and forward.

Occasionally we might say that something is "a matter of style and not of substance," but this is not the sense of the term *style* in Section 3.1. On the contrary, this section contains the themes that underlie virtually all of the remaining sections of the BPM. In fact, if an individual policy in the BPM violates any of the themes in Section 3.1, either the policy must be brought into line with Section 3.1 or there needs to be a good reason for the apparent conflict. For example, in BPM Part 5, "Executive Parameters," you will see a number of specific policies that limit what the CEO can do in several functional areas. These limitations may seem to violate the principle that the board acts strategically and that it leads rather than manages the CEO and the staff. However, the board's guidance to the CEO and the staff is part of the board's ultimate accountability to the stakeholders. Although the board delegates its authority to the CEO, it cannot delegate its fiduciary and legal responsibilities. Accordingly, it must balance its need to fulfill those responsibilities with the commitment to keep its actions at a strategic level. This can be a difficult balance to strike, but we believe that in the process of working through the BPM while keeping Section 3.1 in mind, you will achieve a healthy equilibrium between your strategic thinking and your responsibility to set appropriate boundaries for your CEO.

The specific language shown in the template is similar to that in many BPMs that we have assisted in writing. The list of characteristics is almost identical to the list in *Reinventing the Board* by John Carver,[1] which we have found to be an excellent description of what great boards aspire to. As we suggest earlier, commenting on a board's style may seem academic or even unnecessary. Carver even acknowledges that you "may be tempted to dismiss this policy as motherhood and apple pie . . . but it establishes a required board behavior capable of accomplishing [the organization's mission]."[2] Like Carver, we see this section as being foundational.

As with any of the sample policies in our template, feel free to tailor the language so that you are comfortable with it. We have seen some boards go with a more general statement of style, while others have preferred to be even more prescriptive in Section 3.1. Select the language that best describes the governance style that you want to characterize your board; but in drafting this section, be prepared to make the language more than just talk. You will need to establish procedures that test the board's compliance with this section. For example, saying that the board will be accountable to the stakeholders without backing this up with a way for the board actually to have two-way communication with those stakeholders is dangerous in two ways. First, the board loses the value gained by receiving formal, periodic feedback from its stakeholders. If a board is a representative group of the key stakeholders, the board must find ways to monitor stakeholders' opinions and expectations and to report directly to stakeholders through occasional board reports, surveys, or even phone calls. Second, making these philosophical and style commitments up front is important for recruiting new board members, and even staff, who join the organization with their eyes open to what kind of organization they are joining. A board always wants to be found "walking the talk."

3.2 Board Job Description. The job of the board is to lead the organization toward the desired performance and ensure that that performance occurs. The board's specific contributions are unique to its trusteeship role and necessary for proper governance and management. To perform its job, the board shall:

    3.2.1 Determine the mission, values, strategies, and major goals/outcomes, and hold the CEO accountable for developing a staff strategic plan based on these policies.

    3.2.2 Determine the parameters within which the CEO is expected to achieve the goals/outcomes.

    3.2.3 Monitor the performance of the organization relative to the achievement of the goals/outcomes within the executive parameters.

    3.2.4 Maintain and constantly improve all ongoing policies of the board in this BPM.

    3.2.5 Select, fairly compensate, nurture, evaluate annually, and, if necessary, terminate a CEO, who functions as the board's sole agent.

    3.2.6 Ensure financial solvency and integrity through policies and behavior.

    3.2.7 Require periodic financial and other external audits to ensure compliance with the law and with good practices.

3.2.8 Evaluate and constantly improve our board's performance as the governing board, and set expectations for board members' involvement as volunteers.

The term *job description* can strike people in different ways. For some, a job description is protection; for others, it's a straitjacket. Some may feel that they have too high a position in the organization to have a job description. Their "job" is to accomplish the organization's mission, and its scope should not be limited by detailing the tasks that are involved in the process. Some boards have a similar view about trying to describe the "job" of the board. Yet we have found many boards whose lack of unity and lack of a clear voice are directly attributable to a misunderstanding of their job. The misunderstanding often arises from differing assumptions on the part of board members, the CEO, and the staff. The safest way to avoid a misunderstanding of the board's job is to put a job description in writing in the BPM.

Section 3.2, "Board Job Description," goes hand in hand with Section 3.1, "Governing Style." Together they communicate the board's job and how it will be accomplished. These two sections combine to provide the foundation for the remainder of Part 3 (indeed, for the rest of the BPM) in that all other policies must be consistent with the board's job description and its governance style.

As for the detail in Section 3.2, your board may choose more general descriptors and therefore reduce the list from the eight items shown in the sample BPM, or it may prefer more detail and a longer list. The important point regarding Section 3.2 is that the board deliberates on its role and arrives at a consensus as to what is put into the BPM. You can always change these sections if you find it necessary, but you need to agree on a working draft of these sections and let them guide your thinking throughout the rest of the BPM.

3.3 Board Member Criteria. In nominating members for the board, the board Governance Committee shall be guided by the board profile that is kept current in the Board Reference Book.

This section addresses one of the most important aspects of any board, the criteria for board membership. Your bylaws may include information on the criteria for board members, and you may want to repeat those requirements in BPM Section 3.3. In our experience, few bylaws contain sufficient detail on the qualifications for board membership and on the nomination and election processes. Actually, the BPM is the best place to go into some detail because the desired criteria may change every few years as the organization matures.

In our template, we assume that the bylaws are not prescriptive as to the qualifications for board membership. Notice that, although this is an important consideration for any board, we give it only one sentence in the BPM. However, that one sentence is a reference to what we call a board profile, which is essentially a description of the desired board makeup from various angles.

By thinking through what kind of board will best serve the organization's mission and represent its moral owners, the board is committing itself to make future selections according to a plan that will get it closer to a "dream team." No team can expect to play in the big leagues without careful assessment of where it is and a clear set of guidelines as to where it wants to be in three to five years. We are reminded again that in Jim Collins's *Good to Great,* one of the keys to success is to "get the right people on the bus, get the wrong people off the bus, and put people in the right seats" (our paraphrase). That is the role of a board profile.

Listed in Appendix B is a downloadable handout that you should find helpful in developing a board profile. Because it is a distinct document (and a board policy), the board profile could be embedded directly into Section 3.3 of the BPM. However, we suggest making it an addendum to the BPM and including it as one of the important documents in the "portable board library" that we call the Board Reference Book (see Chapter 11 for more on that governance tool).

In outlining its membership profile for the future, your board can identify specific qualifications and characteristics of its members that are necessary or desirable in order to achieve your mission. It is critical that the entire board agree to the profile and that it direct the nominating group (in the template, we use the governance committee) to be guided by the profile in nominating new board members.

If your bylaws include any necessary or even desirable characteristics of board members, ensure that they are included in your board profile, or change the bylaws if the board does not agree with what is there.

Board profiles vary in specificity and therefore length. They often begin short and grow over time. Good board discussions usually are prompted by the first draft. We like a profile that addresses three questions:

- What qualifications must every candidate have?
- Down the road, what is the board demographic that we think is best for us?
- What specific expertise do we want represented on the board?

These questions suggest a format for your board profile, where you divide the document into three sections, one for each category of criteria.

Category I in the board profile simply lists the "nonnegotiables" for membership on the board; i.e., you would not spend time considering a suggested candidate unless she met these criteria. A religious organization might require membership in its faith community. An environmental group might require a demonstrated commitment to the environment. These qualifications will vary widely, but once you have agreed on the nonnegotiables, honor them and don't compromise.

Category II of the board profile captures the makeup of the total board that you would like to see after a couple more election cycles. There are many potentially divisive issues here. Most boards want more diversity in age, gender, and/or race/ethnicity. Many have the issue of "professional" vs. "layperson." You can decide what the balance should be. Some boards want all of their members to be major donors, while other boards may limit the percentage of members who are major donors. There are lots of options. But we are convinced that boards that are deliberate about choosing new board members move along the good-to-great continuum faster.

Category III of the board profile lists specific areas of expertise that the board determines would benefit its work. A board with seventeen members might list only five such areas. Not every board member needs to fill a specific desired area of expertise. And some board members might bring more than one area. Today, most boards would like to have an attorney as a member. But not just any attorney, we would say. We like specificity, so "an attorney whose clients include at least five nonprofit organizations" is a better descriptor. By the way, that attorney should not also serve as the organization's legal counsel. That would be a conflict of interest, in our opinion. But the attorney on the board contributes legal wisdom to board discussions and advises the board if and when it needs to engage outside legal counsel. Similarly, most non-profit boards want at least one member with financial expertise. But someone in corporate finance who does not understand a non-profit's fund accounting system might not be as valuable as a CPA who audits other nonprofit organizations. Remember, these are "desired" criteria to guide the nomination process, not legally binding definitions.

Even though it may take a while to agree on the contents of the board profile, the board should not consider this to be a static document. Don't let the fact that the board profile is a BPM adden-dum discourage you from keeping it just as current as the main sections of the BPM. Policies and strategies need to change with the times, and the board profile needs to be adjusted accordingly. For example, a board that decides to expand the organization's activities to other countries may want to include a requirement for candidates from those other countries. Similarly, an association that has expanded its membership to include people from different types of organizations may consider changing its board profile to include board members from the recently included organizations.

> **3.4 Orientation.** Prior to election, each nominee shall be given this BPM along with adequate briefings on the role of the board, officers, and staff and an overview of programs, plans, and finances. Soon after election, each new board member will be given more comprehensive orientation material and training.

We have mentioned Jim Collins's principles in *Good to Great* and remarked about how they were being applied to nonprofit organizations. You may recall that after Level 5 Leadership, Collins identified the first step in moving from good to great as being to "get the right people on the bus,"[3] i.e., to identify the kind of people that you want in your organization, recruit them, and only then begin positioning them where they can be most effective. In his study of great companies, Collins pointed out that great companies "hired outstanding people whenever and wherever they found them, often without a specific job in mind."[4]

Nobody can gainsay the critical role of recruiting in building and maintaining a successful team, whether it is playing football, building a jet plane, or governing a nonprofit organization. Let's say that you have completed Section 3.3 of your BPM, including your board profile, and you are satisfied that you have identified and recruited the right people for your board. The next step is to begin to benefit from these people's participation as soon as possible. This means that they need to understand what is expected of them and to be trained to meet those expectations.

Most boards have overlapping terms, so that only a portion of the board is replaced at one time. Whether your new board members come in as a "class" or one at a time to fill individual vacancies, you want them to be contributors right away, or at least we hope you do. We have in fact worked with boards that seem to have an unwritten assumption that new board members need time to acclimate themselves to the board, or even "pay their dues" before their opinions are given weight. While these boards may deny that this is the assumption, their lack of a good and early orientation program suggests otherwise.

The value of an effective orientation program is hardly a revelation to anyone who is at all acquainted with good governance. Nor is it difficult to find good references on how to design and deliver an orientation program. A recent Google search for "orienting a nonprofit board" resulted in 122,000 references. Although we cannot vouch for the value of all of the references, there is plenty there for any board that is committed to orienting and training its new members. What we can vouch for, however, is the value of the BPM in the orientation process.

Notice that in Section 3.4 of the template, the policy is not only to orient and train newly elected board members, but also to orient prospective candidates prior to their election. This is important, as it allows candidates to understand what is required of board members before they are appointed or before they stand for election. It is especially important in the nonprofit world, where board members are typically volunteers. Nothing we know of provides a clearer message to a new or prospective board member than the succinct articulation and comprehensive summary of board policies that resides in the BPM. Thirty minutes with the BPM is usually sufficient for a prospective candidate to understand what will be expected of him if he should come onto the board. Besides, if a candidate goes through your preelection orientation and decides that a three-year term is really not what he wants to do, the board has just saved itself an unhappy experience with that person. As the saying goes, "The best time to fire a person is before he is hired."

We do not include a description of the orientation and training program in the BPM because we prefer that it simply be incorporated by reference, as shown in BPM Section 3.4. You many want to include it as an addendum to the BPM similar to the board profile, but you should also maintain it in the Board Reference Book.[5] Board orientation and training is usually the purview of the governance committee, which oversees the performance of the board, develops and delivers the orientation of new members, and conducts the ongoing training of the board.

3.5 Chair's Role. The job of the chair is, primarily, to maintain the integrity of the board's processes. The chair "manages the board." The chair is the only board member authorized to speak for the board, other than in rare and specifically board-authorized instances.

The chair ensures that the board behaves in a manner consistent with its own rules and those legitimately imposed upon it from outside the organization. Meeting discussion content will be those issues that, according to board policy, clearly belong to the board to decide, not to staff.

The authority of the chair consists only in making decisions on behalf of the board that fall within and are consistent with any reasonable interpretation of board policies in Parts 3 and 4 of this BPM. The chair has no authority to make decisions beyond policies created by the board. Therefore, the chair has no authority to supervise or direct the CEO's work, but is expected to maintain close communication with, offer advice to, and provide encouragement to the CEO and staff on behalf of the board.

Among nonprofits that we've seen, no position in the organization is subject to wider interpretation than that of the chair. At one extreme, we have seen chairs who virtually run the organization: they set policy by themselves, supervise the staff, and look to the rest of the board to support them in their role as a do-it-all-guy. At the other extreme are the chairs who exercise modest leadership, show little initiative, and generally stay out of the way. In describing the chair, we have heard board members use terms like *dynamic, lazy, control freak, hands-off leader, overbearing, timid, committed, blasé, confident,* and *self-centered*. Seldom do we hear that the chair is a "good manager." Yet, as described in Section 3.5, that is the chair's role—to be a good manager of the board.

We have found some chairs and even some board members who chafe at the notion of being a "manager" of the board. Typically, those who are asked to chair nonprofit boards are strong leaders, some of them quite prominent in their areas. They don't like to be called mere managers. But that, of course, is not what we mean. There is nothing "mere" about the role of the chair. It's the chair's job to ensure that the board operates with integrity vis-à-vis the rules that it has laid out for itself. Done right, this is one of the truly key assignments for boards that are committed to excellence.

Establishing the chair as the manager of the board is a healthy way to portray the position. It identifies the chair's position as a job and not just an award to recognize a deed, a large donation, or a person's high profile in the community. When the chair is seen as the manager of the board, she can be elected on qualities like fairness, being an effective facilitator of group dynamics, and being a guardian of the board's culture. Yes, it should be considered an honor to serve as chair, but selecting a person as chair on a basis other than her competence in managing the board runs the risk of getting a mediocre chair and frustrated board members. Finally, this approach to the role of the chair encourages board members to be active and influential participants and not simply to wait to hear what the chair has to say before giving their opinion on an issue. If you have good board members who meet the profile that you want for your board, then elect a chair who will bring out their value. Because this role is so important, we advise boards to elect a chair annually, evaluate her performance, and reelect her as long as her performance is high and she is eligible to serve on the board. Passing the assignment around just to allow more board members the chance to wear the mantle of chair is not good practice.

On the list of downloadable material in Appendix B is a short summary of the role of the chair of a nonprofit board.

3.6 Board Meetings. Board events often will include time for guest presenters, interaction with staff and beneficiaries, board training, and social activities, as well as business sessions. Policies that are intended to improve the process for planning and running meetings follow:

3.6.1. The schedule for board meetings shall be set two years in advance.

3.6.2. The CEO shall work with the chair and the committee chairs in developing agendas, which, along with background materials for the board and committees, monitoring reports, the CEO's recommendations for changes in the BPM, previous minutes, and other such materials, shall be mailed to all board members approximately two weeks in advance of board meetings.

3.6.3 Minutes and the updated BPM shall be sent to board members within 14 days of board meetings.

3.6.4 Regular board meetings shall be held ___ times a year in the months of _____, _____, and _____, preceded by a reminder notice approximately 30 days in advance of the meeting date. The _____ meeting shall include a review of the planning and budgeting for the upcoming year. The _____ meeting shall include a review of the performance of the CEO and the organization for the past year. Special meetings of the board can be called according to the bylaws [if this process is not in the bylaws, define it here].

3.6.5 The Governance Committee shall prepare a meeting evaluation form for completion by each board member who attends the board meeting. The completed forms shall be reviewed, analyzed, and summarized by the Governance Committee, which shall report the results of the meeting evaluation to the board members within two weeks of the board meeting.

The frequency of board meetings among nonprofits varies from once or twice a year to once a month. Among the organizations we have worked with, the median is three to four meetings a year. Although the bylaws may contain instructions on meetings, they are normally limited to the obligation to have an annual meeting, who can call a special meeting, the lead time and related requirements for both regular and special meetings, and other features that may be required by the state.

Our thoughts about the frequency of board meetings are summarized in a downloadable document listed in Appendix B.

BPM Section 3.6 addresses the subject of board meetings from the standpoint of both administration and substance. From an administrative perspective, Section 3.6 makes clear such matters as:

- When the meetings will be held
- When reminders and read-ahead materials will be sent to board members before the meeting
- When minutes will be distributed after the meeting
- Other instructions that the board believes should apply

With respect to the substance of the meetings, we like to see the BPM reflect:

- The importance of meetings in reinforcing the board's culture as well as its business of governing
- The process by which agendas are set
- The purpose of each regularly scheduled meeting
- How read-ahead materials should be prepared and distributed
- How the board will systematically evaluate the quality and effectiveness of its meetings
- Other areas of substance that the board wants to see in its meetings

You want Section 3.6 to give the reader a clear idea of what is expected of a board member in terms of frequency and content of board meetings. You may choose to repeat language from the bylaws in Section 3.6 so that the BPM will be complete in its instructions regarding regularly scheduled meetings, but normally a simple reference will suffice. Notice in Section 3.6.4 that for special meetings, we direct the reader to the bylaws.

Section 3.6.1 shows that the schedule of meetings is to be set two years in advance. This may seem too prescriptive for some boards, but attendance improves and staff planning is better if everyone knows the dates and times of meetings this far in advance. Give plenty of notice as to the location of the meeting as well. The sooner your board members know the dates and locations of board meetings, the less likely they are to plead a schedule conflict.

Much has been and will be said about the quality of board meetings, and we don't have the space to discuss how you make your meetings relevant, interesting, informative, and even fun. With a Google search on "running efficient board meetings" revealing over 11 million links, we do not believe that you need more preaching on this subject. What we will say is that boards that (1) adopt a governance style (BPM Section 3.1) and (2) know their jobs (BPM Section 3.2) will have a head start in making meetings valuable. The key is to think of a meeting as an event that you want to be memorable and productive. Most boards plan time for board members to get to know one another better; to learn something about the organization or about governance; to meet in committees, unless that is done between board dates; to have "action-free time" to explore new issues or dream five years out; and, of course, to meet in plenary session to act on policy options.

Although many local boards try monthly one-hour meetings, there are always some people who show up late and some who leave early, creating a sense of rush under pressure rather than a more thoughtful, deliberative environment. We like there to be at least one board retreat each year, primarily to allow board members to get to know one another and to think longer-term than most meetings allow. Generally, fewer but longer meetings are better than many short meetings. If the board has an executive committee, that group can always act if an emergency arises between meetings.

The list in Appendix B includes a downloadable handout that summarizes our thoughts on good board meetings.

3.7 Standing Committees. Committees help the board be effective and efficient. They speak "to the board" and not "for the board." Unless authorized by the whole board, a committee may not exercise authority that is reserved to the whole board by the bylaws or by the laws of [*name of state*] governing not-for-profit organizations. Committees are not created to advise or exercise authority over staff. Once committees are created by the board, the board chair shall recommend committee chairs and members for one-year terms, subject to board approval. The board chair and the CEO are *ex officio* members of all committees except the Audit and Compliance Committee. The CEO shall assign one senior staff member to assist with the work of each committee.

Some (small) boards work just fine without committees, choosing to take care of everything in plenary sessions. However, much if not most of the "work" of many boards is done in their standing committees, which are those committees that have an ongoing function in the governance structure. Later in this chapter, we discuss the individual standing committees that we have included in the template, but in this opening paragraph of BPM Section 3.7, we establish a few principles for the standing committees.

The most fundamental principle for board committees is that they speak *to* the board and not *for* the board. The committee is not a mini-board in the sense that it can make policy on its own. To be sure, it should oversee the policies in its particular functional area, and when it comes time to develop a policy in its area, it should be the most influential voice in the boardroom. For example, the board should look to the finance committee to formulate policies pertaining to such matters as approval authority for purchases, expense reimbursement policies, and the policies for periodic financial reporting to the board. But language that is drafted in committee does not become policy until it is approved by the whole board.

"Speaking to the board and not for the board" also means that the committee does not enjoy the right to supervise the staff once policies are adopted. That's the job of the CEO. Remember that the BPM is the single voice of the board to the CEO. We have seen too many boards that have given committees tacit (or explicit) license to supervise the staff in their functional area, a practice that usually ends up with little compartments of control, or "silos." The single voice of the board becomes a cacophony that is frustrating to the CEO, the staff, and the board members themselves.

Because the committees work for the board, the board determines the number and scope of the committees. Each standing committee is then identified and described generally in a section under the "Standing Committees" section in the BPM. In our template (Section 3.7), we state that the board chair selects the committee chairs and populates the committees, with both actions being subject to approval by the board. Authorizing the chair to form the committees and name their chairs recognizes his role as the manager of the board and facilitates the process. Committee membership changes often, and the board chair is in the best position to effect the change most efficiently. These appointments need to reflect experience, personal preference, balance, expected major issues, input from the CEO and staff who will be working with committee chairs, and other such information. This takes some up-front thinking, a few phone calls and e-mails, and possibly some personal meetings over several days before making the committee assignments.

Section 3.7 includes language that applies generally to standing committees, such as the fact that the chair and CEO are *ex officio* members of all committees except the audit committee.[6] You may want to include other general requirements, e.g., that committees can include non-board members. This is often helpful to small boards and can be a good way to prepare future board members. If this is done, the BPM may specify that a majority of the committee members should be board members. Other BPM provisions can address committee reports, frequency of meetings, and other such areas.

Of course, these are merely items to consider for Section 3.7.

Requirements that pertain to specific committees are included in the appropriate sections under Section 3.7. We typically do not list members of individual committees in the BPM because they change so frequently. We recommend that a current board organization chart, including an updated list of committee members, be kept in the Board Reference Book (see Chapter 11). Two important questions that often arise with regard to committees are:

1. **Should we repeat bylaw language?** Your bylaws may contain a section on committees and may even name specific committees that must be maintained. Although we prefer merely to refer to the bylaws and not repeat the language in the BPM, for this section we find that having all the committee information in one place justifies repeating the actual text of the bylaws or a paraphrase of that text. Because we believe that (1) committees are only tools that a board uses to be more effective and (2) the number and functions of committees may change over a period of a few years, we prefer that the bylaws simply state that "the board may form such committees as it may determine."

2. **How Many Committees?** We are frequently asked whether there are rules of thumb as to the number and type of committees that an organization should have. As to the number of committees, we remind boards that committees are easier to form than to kill. Accordingly, when starting out, err on the side of having too few committees. For example, even though the functions of finance and investment may call for different skills, you may want to start with one finance committee and separate it into two committees only after you see that this is warranted by the workload. As for the types of committees that we typically recommend, those included in Subsections 3.7.1 through 3.7.5 are committees that are common to most nonprofits.

Finally, the reference in Section 3.7 to staff support conveys the message that, although the committees don't supervise staff, they are entitled to receive staff support to prepare information and materials for their agendas.

The list in Appendix B includes a downloadable summary of our thoughts on board standing committees.

> ***3.7.1 Governance Committee.*** This committee shall recommend policies to the board pertaining to governance issues and processes, including the orientation and training of new board members, the evaluation and improvement of the contribution of individual board members and officers, and the recommendation of bylaw changes. The committee will also develop a roster of potential board members based on the board profile, and will nominate all board members and officers.

The board has many roles and functions, as have been listed in BPM Section 3.2. Its overall job, however, is to govern. As obvious as that statement is, you might be surprised by the number of boards that don't dedicate a committee to oversee the board's performance as a governing body. The governance committee's role is to orient, train, evaluate, and encourage. It is the coach, teacher, and counselor in the area of board structure and processes. It brings objectivity and clarity to the governance function and ensures that this function is given the weight that it deserves.

As important as this committee is to the board, of the six committees that we have selected for the template, the governance committee is the one that is most likely to be missing from a nonprofit board. Some boards believe that the bylaws are clear enough on how the organization is to be governed and that they don't need a special committee to focus on their own work. For small boards with little turnover in their membership, the chair often oversees the governance function. While this approach may be efficient, it also has trouble adjusting as the organization grows. The median size of nonprofit boards is in the range of fifteen to seventeen members. Although there is no magic threshold for when you need a governance committee, any board of over ten or twelve members probably needs the focus and objectivity of a governance committee.

This committee is sometimes called the board development committee because of its role in board orientation and training. The names "governance" and "board development" both have the potential for being misunderstood. A governance committee, for example, can be seen as having the role of governing, rather than the role of advising on governance structure and process. Giving this committee the label "board development," however, can lead it to be confused with the more common use of the word *development*, i.e., fund-raising.

While we have no strong preference concerning the name of this committee, we recommend that it receive careful attention from your board. Select a chair for this committee who enjoys the respect of the other members and who is not afraid to challenge them, or in some cases recommend discipline. If you have policies and standards for board members' performance, someone needs to enforce them. Usually that role falls to the governance committee. This can be particularly tricky for a nonprofit with volunteer board members, many of whom are your largest donors. If you don't intend to hold board members to certain standards of performance, don't set the standards to begin with. If you do have standards that you expect to be followed, look to your governance committee to help your members respect them. In that vein, therefore, organize and populate your governance committee so that it is viewed more as a coach than as a policeman.

3.7.2 Finance Committee. This committee shall develop and recommend to the board those financial principles, plans, and courses of action that provide for mission accomplishment and organizational financial well-being. Consistent with this responsibility, it shall review the annual budget and submit it to the board for its approval. In addition, the committee shall make recommendations with regard to the level and terms of indebtedness, cash management, investment policy, risk management, financial monitoring and reports, employee benefit plans, signatory authority for expenditures, and other policies for inclusion in the BPM that the committee determines are advisable for effective financial management.

Almost all boards have a finance committee, although the scope of this committee varies widely among nonprofits. Note that this committee, like the others, does not set policy, but only studies the issues in more detail, then recommends policies to the full board. Smaller boards will tend to give this committee wide latitude, as is articulated in our template, where the finance committee handles all aspects of financial management: budgeting, accounting, investing, reporting, employee benefits, and the financial audit. Boards with larger and more complicated finances may separate some of these functions and possibly have a separate investment committee and a different small group for the audit committee. Because so much regulatory attention is focused on the independence of the audit function, many nonprofits are separating the audit function from the finance committee. Accordingly, our template shows a separate audit and compliance committee.

As with the governance committee, the board chair should give special attention to the leadership and membership of the finance committee. Most nonprofits have a board member or members with financial management skills. Obviously, here is where you want them. However, although we assume that boards will look to members with financial skills and experience to sit on the finance committee, we do not recommend that you choose your committee chair strictly on his financial expertise. Yes, the chair of the finance committee needs to be able to understand the financial issues that arise, but he also needs to be able to communicate them to the rest of the board. Too often, reports from the finance committee are met with blank looks of misunderstanding or, worse, indifference, because members can't interpret the data. The board may defer to the finance committee on financial matters, but it cannot delegate its fiduciary responsibility to the committee. Ensure, therefore, that the finance committee takes seriously its responsibility of working with the board to bring financial data to the board that are accurate and complete, but also clear and able to be acted upon by the board.

> **3.7.3 Audit and Compliance Committee.** This committee shall oversee the organization's internal accounting controls; recommend external auditors for board approval; review the external auditors' annual audit plan; and review the annual report, the management letter, and the results of the external audit. The committee, or its delegate, shall have an annual private conversation with the auditor. In addition, the committee shall be responsible for oversight of regulatory compliance, policies and practices regarding corporate responsibility, and ethics and business conduct–related activities, including compliance with all federal, state, and local laws governing tax-exempt entities. The committee shall also oversee written conflict of interest policies and procedures for directors and officers (see tab __ of the Board Reference Book).

Just as the governance committee lends objectivity to the evaluation of the board's structure and processes, the audit and compliance committee lends objectivity to the assessment of the organization's financial integrity. Most of the scandals that have occurred in both the for-profit and nonprofit worlds could have been prevented, or at least greatly lessened, had the board been more diligent in carrying out its oversight duties. The Sarbanes-Oxley Act of 2002 (the Act) introduced a long list of audit and disclosure requirements, which are only now becoming routine in the for-profit environment. Although the Act does not cover nonprofit organizations, many nonprofit boards, particularly boards of larger organizations, are adopting several of its principles. For example, the Act requires that public companies have a "financial expert" on their audit committee, and many nonprofit boards have imposed that requirement on themselves.[7]

3.7.4 Advancement Committee. This committee shall study and recommend policies relating to communications and public relations as well as policies relating to raising financial and other resources for the organization.

Because almost all nonprofits depend on contributions for their success, their ability to attract financial support is critical. There are dozens of ways to appeal to donors and encourage them to invest in your organization. Your development strategy is probably based on the mission and culture of your organization, its brand or reputation, the profile of your donor base, your reliance on government funding, or other factors influencing your relationship with your donors. Whatever your development strategy, however, it must be (1) tied into your overall strategy for the organization and (2) solidly owned by the board.

Donors generally occupy a high rung on the ladder of stakeholders of nonprofit organizations. Therefore, boards can be rather fussy about how donors are treated. The policies that the board develops are designed to guide the CEO and staff on such matters as permissible methods of fund-raising and acceptable methods of communicating with donors. The board may also want to set policies for how its directors may be employed for pay in fund-raising (or other) activities apart from their governance work. These types of policies normally will be brought forward to the full board by the advancement committee. You may want to be more explicit in your description of the scope of the advancement committee than we have been in the template. For example, you may want to enumerate the types of communication that are within the scope of the advancement committee. Some boards prefer to separate oversight of fund-raising (development) from media and public relations, marketing, communications systems, and other such areas and have two separate committees. Because the message and brand of a nonprofit need to be consistent in all these areas, we prefer to have them all covered by one advancement committee.

3.7.5 Programs Committee. This committee shall study and recommend policies relating to all programs and services of the organization.

Programs" is a generic label for one or many activities that the organization undertakes to achieve its mission. Again, the committee studies the issues in more depth from a policy perspective, avoiding any supervisory role over the staff running the programs. The committee is looking for "parameters" around each of the major programs, within which the board asks its CEO and staff to make professional choices about the whole range of decisions necessary for effective and efficient operations. As an example of how committee assignments should be flexible, a small organization might include fund-raising for programs among the responsibilities of its program committee. However, a complex organization, say a university, might choose to break up "programs" into several separate committees for academic affairs, student affairs, health sciences, and so on. It is difficult to prejudge such decisions.

A cautionary note: We encourage the board to set broad policies regarding its various programs. We don't advocate forming a committee for every program, a practice that we have seen in some organizations. Such a practice can lead to inconsistent, conflicting, and overly detailed policies. Keeping the program committee high and broad in its viewpoint will help ensure that individual programs are coordinated, consistently and objectively evaluated, and eliminated when they are no longer effective.

3.7.6 Executive Committee. This committee shall comprise the chair, other officers, and the chairs of the other committees in Section 3.7. Except for the actions enumerated below, it shall have the authority to act for the board on all matters so long as the Executive Committee determines that it would be imprudent to wait for the next board meeting to take such action. With respect to any action taken on behalf of the board, (1) the Executive Committee is required to report the action to the board within 10 days, and (2) the board must approve the action at the next board meeting.

The Executive Committee is not authorized to make decisions or to take action with respect to the following matters:

3.7.6.1 Dissolving the corporation

3.7.6.2 Hiring or firing the chief executive

3.7.6.3 Entering into major contracts or suing another entity

3.7.6.4 Making significant changes to a board-approved budget

3.7.6.5 Adopting or eliminating major programs

3.7.6.6 Buying or selling property

3.7.6.7 Amending the bylaws

3.7.6.8 Changing any policies that the board determines may be changed only by the board

Why Have an Executive Committee?

The primary purpose of an executive committee is to increase the efficiency of the governance process by acting for the board between meetings. It is often difficult to assemble the board to address matters that require quick decisions and actions. Executive committees, therefore, are common among boards that:

- Are large.
- Are geographically diverse.
- Meet infrequently.
- Are in transition or crisis.
- Require frequent legal actions.

These criteria are not carved in stone, and just because one or more of these factors applies to your board does not mean that you need an executive committee. Take, for example, the issue of size. When is a board large enough to warrant an executive committee? In its booklet on the executive committee, BoardSource offers the following guidelines:

- *Fewer than 13 members:* An executive committee is probably not needed.
- *Between 13 and 23 members:* An executive committee can be helpful for a narrow range of board duties and actions.
- *More than 23 members:* An executive committee can be helpful for a broad range of board actions.

Technology improvements over the past ten years have tended to weaken the argument for having an executive committee. For example, the widespread use of mobile communication and the availability of inexpensive and good-quality conference call vendors have increased the ability of boards to meet by telephone, thereby reducing the need for an executive committee.

Some boards will use the executive committee as a sounding board, i.e., a subset of board members who can efficiently screen issues prior to presenting them to the entire board. In a similar role, an executive committee may be used to review and approve the agendas for board meetings. We don't disagree with this use of an executive committee, but it can often lead to a two-tiered board, which, as we discuss later in this chapter, is a characteristic that is seldom found in good boards, let alone great ones.

If the executive committee is mentioned in the bylaws, of course, your BPM will need to be consistent with the instructions in the bylaws. Your bylaws may even list who is on the executive committee. We prefer to leave the size and configuration of all committees to the BPM by stating in the bylaws that the board may establish those committees that it considers necessary to carry out its duties. Accordingly, if you have the authority to change the bylaws, we recommend amending them to take out any details concerning the executive committee. For that matter, we prefer that the bylaws not even mention an executive committee, thereby giving your board the flexibility to decide whether to have one at all.

Who Sits on an Executive Committee?

Normally, as shown in the template, the committee comprises the chair and other officers plus the chairs of the various standing committees. The board chair is almost always the chair of the executive committee. In identifying the members of your executive committee, keep in mind that one of the key reasons for this committee to exist is the greater efficiency of a smaller group. Don't overload your executive committee unnecessarily or use assignment to the committee simply as a status symbol. You want a streamlined committee made up of board members who are both available and willing to give extra time and attention to the board. Usually no more than 20 to 25 percent of the board should serve on the executive committee.

Executive Committee Limitations and Requirements

Although the executive committee is usually given broad authority to make decisions for the board, is it good practice to make clear what authority is being granted. Notice that in the template, we suggest a general limitation: Before the executive committee can assume any authority to make a decision, it must determine that it would be imprudent to wait for the next board meeting to take such action. Moreover, the BPM requires that any time the executive committee takes action on behalf of the board, it must report that action to the full board within ten days and then have the board approve the action at the next board meeting.

In Sections 3.7.6.1 through 3.7.6.8, we itemize the specific decisions that the executive committee is proscribed from making on behalf of the board. These general and specific limitations are fairly standard for those boards that have executive committees, but we have seen examples of executive committees with substantially fewer restrictions (i.e., more authority) and, conversely, examples where the executive committee is given only modest authority to act for the full board. Each board with an executive committee must decide how much authority it will delegate.

Executive Committee Meetings

Just as board meetings require adequate preparation to ensure that they are run efficiently, so it is with executive committee meetings. Because there are fewer participants in these meetings, there sometimes is a tendency to "wing it" and not give the meeting the planning it deserves. Yet the requirement that the executive committee report its actions to the full board and later have those actions ratified puts pressure on the organization of executive committee meetings and the documentation coming out of them. Accordingly, you may want to include in this section some language about the preparation of advance materials, requirements for comprehensive minutes, clarity of documentation and reporting, and so on.

The Risk of Having an Executive Committee

In this book, we have stated many times in many ways that the board should think of itself as a unit. We also have emphasized the importance of leveraging the different skills and perspectives of the individual board members. Boards with executive committees must be careful to avoid giving the idea that there is more than one class of board membership. It is not unusual for an executive committee to become the de facto board, in that it vets all the important issues and other board members are relegated to the role of ratifying the committee's decisions or recommendations. It is difficult to motivate board members who think of themselves as being in the second tier. Even if the executive committee is simply being used as a sounding board, the unspoken message to the rest of the board members may be that they must wait to be told by the executive committee whether an issue is worth their time and attention.

The language in Part 3 of your BPM relating to the style of your board and its commitment to speaking with one voice, combined with clear policies relating to the role of and limitations on the executive committee, will allow you to gain the benefits of efficiency while reducing the risk of having a two-tiered board. You want all of your board members to be engaged to take full advantage of the talent you have taken pains to recruit.

3.7.7 Other committees as determined.

There is no shortage of material on how to form committees and define their scope.[8] You can find techniques for committee structures and descriptions of individual committees. The number of committees used by your board will depend on such factors as the size of your board and the complexity of your organization. Our inclusion of five committees plus an executive committee is not intended to prescribe the specific number of committees for your board. Although we advise initially keeping the number of committees small, you may choose to create other standing committees if the committee process is producing good results. Often, however, new issues that come up can be assigned to a short-term, ad hoc task force, which we address next.

3.8 Advisory Groups, Councils, and Task Forces.

To increase its knowledge base and depth of available expertise, the board supports the use of groups, councils, and task forces of qualified advisers. The term *council* refers to a group that (1) is created and approved by the board and (2) provides ongoing advice and counsel to the CEO or the board. The term "task force" refers to any group appointed by the CEO or the chair to assist him or her in carrying out various time-limited goals and responsibilities. Although either the chair or the CEO may form a task force, he or she shall notify the board of its formation, purpose, and membership within 10 days of its formation. The CEO may assign a senior staff member to serve advisory groups. The board has established the following advisory groups:

3.8.1 (Name, membership, function, etc., of any advisory group the board creates.)

Many nonprofit organizations have advisory groups populated by individuals whose perspective or expertise is valued by the board. Usually these advisory groups have no decision-making authority, but rather are called upon by the board to offer counsel on a particular issue or policy that requires input beyond board members' expertise. These councils usually are listed in the BPM along with their purpose and makeup. The language in the BPM template points out that councils work for the board and are therefore established by the board. This is in contrast with task forces, which may be established by either the CEO or the board chair to address specific problems or issues. While an advisory council can be ongoing, task forces are time-limited, usually disbanding after their task is completed.

Advisory councils can serve as excellent resources for a board in that they can provide valuable input and two-way communication between the board and stakeholders. If you have an advisory council, ensure that its role is clearly spelled out in the BPM. If it's not, whatever value it may bring you may be offset by the confusion in roles and frustration on the part of both council members and board members.

3.9 Board Members' Code of Conduct. The board expects of itself and its members ethical and businesslike conduct. Board members must offer unconflicted loyalty to the interests of the entire organization, superseding any conflicting loyalty such as that to family members, advocacy or interest groups, and other boards or staffs of which they are members. The board members must avoid any conflict of interest with respect to their fiduciary responsibility. There must be no self-dealing or conduct of private business or personal services between any board member and the organization except as procedurally controlled to assure openness, competitive opportunity, and equal access to "inside" information.

The board will make no judgments of the CEO or staff performance except as the performance of the CEO is assessed against explicit board policies and agreed-upon performance objectives.

Each board member is expected to complete and sign an Annual Affirmation Statement, which covers, *inter alia*, board conflicts of interest, in accordance with the laws of the state governing not-for-profit organizations, and other expectations of board members.

This section contains a summary of what a board expects of its members in terms of their ethical behavior. In the first paragraph of Section 3.9, the board makes a general statement to the effect that individual members are expected to park any personal or financial conflicts outside the boardroom door and participate as people who are fully dedicated to the organization's success.

The second paragraph reiterates the point that the CEO works for the board, not for any individual board member. The paragraph is also a reminder that board members are expected to honor their commitment to confidentiality with respect to board matters in general and the board's evaluation of the CEO in particular. Few things undermine the board–CEO relationship faster than individual board members having individual agendas for the CEO that differ from the objectives explicitly laid out for the CEO by the full board.

The third paragraph of this section mentions an Annual Affirmation Statement, a sample of which is shown in Figure 8-1. Many boards find this statement a helpful way for their members, on an annual, automatic schedule, to consider what is being asked of them for the coming year. Especially when terms run for multiple years, there is an assumption that every member of the board is willing to exert the effort necessary to be an effective participant on the board. Sometimes board members have an issue at home or at work that will affect their ability to serve on the board. The Annual Affirmation Statement can give them a chance to assess that issue and either reaffirm their continued commitment for another year or communicate graciously that they cannot do justice to their position as a board member.

The items in this form as shown in Figure 8-1 are fairly standard, but you should include only those that apply to your board. For example, some boards do not require their members to be contributors of record, as we suggest in Item 3. (See also Section 3.10 of the template.) Also, some boards expect their board mem-

FIGURE 8-1.

ANNUAL AFFIRMATION STATEMENT

(Please consider thoughtfully, sign, and return in the envelope provided.)

1. I continue to support our mission, purpose, and leadership.

2. I understand board membership requires the equivalent of __ days per year of my time, including preparation and meetings. I am able to give that time during the twelve months ahead and expect to attend all board and committee meetings unless I give the chairman advance notice of my need to be absent for good cause.

3. I intend to contribute financially to our organization during the year and will help open doors to friends who may be interested in contributing.

4. I have reviewed and intend to comply with our board Conflict of Interest policy as stated in _____ [reference to the version and location of your Conflict of Interest Statement].

5. [Add other items important to your board]

6. If anything should occur during the year that would prevent me from keeping these intentions of being a positive contributor to our board, I will take the initiative to speak with the officers about a voluntary resignation to allow another to serve who is able to meet these expectations of all board members.

____ I am able to affirm all of the above items and look forward to continued service.

____ Given my current circumstances, I am unable to affirm all of the above and request that the board accept my resignation effective _____ and seek a replacement who can meet all expectations of board members.

Signed: _____ Date: _____

bers to contribute a certain number of volunteer hours each year. Those expectations would become items on the Annual Affirmation Statement. Because most boards already have a Conflict of Interest Statement, we simply reference it in Item 4 of Figure 8-1. We have seen some boards combine the Annual Affirmation and Conflict of Interest statements into one document that board members sign each year.

Some boards we have worked with feel that it is a little much to ask their members to reassert their willingness to keep serving. They have enough trouble getting good people to be on the board, and they don't want to discourage any members from staying on for another year.

We sympathize with the concern for retaining key or high-profile board members and not offending them, but we believe that the Annual Affirmation Statement is an appropriate way to have board members renew their commitments to the board and set aside the necessary time in their schedules. In addition to providing for a recommitment, the Annual Affirmation Statement underscores the seriousness with which you take board membership. Besides, if the requirement for an Annual Affirmation Statement is in the BPM before the board member agrees to serve, she should take no offense at signing it each year. Strong board members value procedures that keep the bar high—both for getting on and for remaining on good boards.

Above all, be consistent in your requirement for the Annual Affirmation Statement. Have it apply to all board members. If you have an important board member who does not want to sign the statement, you may be reluctant to push him for fear that he will leave the board. The risk you run, however, is the creation of a two-tiered board: those who commit to the job and those who are too important to make the commitment. It's better to put the high-profile, low-commitment person on an advisory committee where he can be associated with your organization, but where he can do less damage to the unity of the board.

In summary, we have seen the Annual Affirmation Statement used effectively without its being perceived as bureaucratic or offensive to board members. If it's in the BPM and prospective board members read it and agree to serve, they are likely to value a board that takes its role seriously. The clear benefit to the board is a renewed sense of commitment from all board members and an understanding that they are expected to give the time and attention required to make this a great board. They may be on other boards that make fewer demands on their members' time, but for your board, they are expected to do their job. It's a high standard, but high standards bring out the best of people and the best in people.

> **3.10 Board Finances.** Every board member is expected to be a donor of record in each calendar year. Expenses incurred to fulfill board activities normally can be an individual tax deduction; however, any board member may submit for reimbursement any expenses incurred to attend board or committee meetings.

It is not uncommon for members of a nonprofit board to be among the top donors to the organization, since the level of financial contribution is certainly a key indicator of a donor's enthusiasm for the organization. We know of boards that expect their members to make their organization one of the top two or three recipients of the members' charitable giving.

Some boards are explicit about their expectations of board members, but, sadly, too many are not. Out of courtesy to everyone involved and because this is a sensitive area, it is an area where you want to be clear—especially with boards that have a highly diverse profile of members. Although BPM Section 3.10 states plainly that board members are expected to be donors of record, it does not specify an amount. This allows the board members to give an amount that they think is appropriate. Each board can judge how board members are likely to interpret the policy. Of course, if your board has a threshold contribution for board members, put that amount in your BPM. We have also seen boards specify an amount for the minimum expected contribution. Some boards believe that contributions should be a matter of conscience only and not a requirement for board membership. Other boards believe that having it on the record that all board members are contributors sends the right signal to the public in general and the staff in particular. Here again, your board can determine what is appropriate for your organization.

Regarding the reimbursement of expenses, we also find a variance among boards, with some reimbursing board members as a matter of course and others expecting their board members to cover their own expenses. This latter policy can reduce the pool of candidates for board membership to only those who can afford to cover their expenses and may at the same time favor candidates who are geographically close to the normal board meeting location. This is probably not a bias that you want to impose on your selection process, and you may at least offer reimbursement if a board member requests it, as we have done in BPM Section 3.10. This approach reduces the bias based on income and geography, so long as the policy is honored without prejudice, i.e., there is no stigma attached to requests for reimbursement.

✧

Committing to the principles expressed in Part 3 signals to everyone in an organization that the board wants excellence throughout. People gravitate toward success, not toward mediocrity. Good boards set high standards and meet them. Part 3 of the BPM is the place to document those standards and expectations. Once the board agrees on its own structure and process, it is ready to set policies concerning how it wants to relate to its "one agent," the chief executive officer, and the staff. That is the topic of the next chapter.

CHAPTER 9

BPM Part 4: Board–CEO/Staff Relationship

The most important relationship in governance is that between the board and the CEO. As such, it deserves this separate part of the BPM to ensure that the roles and responsibilities of the CEO and the staff in relationship to the board are crystal clear. The board is responsible for hiring the CEO, supporting her throughout her term of office, and evaluating her fairly on a regular basis. Supporting her involves providing both adequate resources and sufficient authority. Just as the board has a single voice when "speaking" (the BPM), so, too, it has a single agent (the CEO) to act on its behalf.

The preceding paragraph is a summary of BPM Part 4, which contains those policies that the board believes will clarify its partnership with its CEO and provide guidance to the staff as a whole. The first three parts of the BPM lead naturally to this topic in that they establish the BPM as the board's one voice (Part 1), set the strategic direction of the organization (Part 2), and describe the board's structure and processes (Part 3). Now, in BPM Part 4, we see the board document its partner relationship with the CEO. Again, our template and comments flow from our experience with this Part 4, but they should not limit your use of your own philosophy and insights to improve on the language to best fit your situation.

4.1 Delegation to the Chief Executive Officer (CEO).
While the board's job is generally confined to establishing high-level policies, implementation and subsidiary policy development are delegated to the CEO.

4.1.1 All board authority delegated to staff is delegated through the CEO, so that all authority and accountability of staff—as far as the board is concerned—is considered to be the authority and accountability of the CEO.

4.1.2 Organization Essentials policies (Part 2) direct the CEO to achieve certain results. Executive Parameters policies (Part 5) define the acceptable boundaries of prudence and ethics within which the CEO is expected to operate. The CEO is authorized to establish all further policies, make all decisions, take all actions, and develop all activities as long as they are consistent with any reasonable interpretation of the board's policies in this BPM.

4.1.3 The board may change its policies during any meeting, thereby shifting the boundary between board and CEO domains. Consequently, the board may change the latitude of choice given to the CEO, but so long as any particular delegation is in place, the board and its members will respect and support the CEO's choices. This does not prevent the board from obtaining information in the delegated areas.

4.1.4 Except when a person or committee has been authorized by the board to incur some amount of staff cost for study of an issue, no board member, officer, or committee has authority over the CEO. Only officers or committee chairs may request information, but if such a request—in the CEO's judgment—requires a material amount of staff time or funds or is disruptive, it may be refused.

A first reading of Section 4.1 and its supporting paragraphs in the template may suggest that the board could delegate some of its authority to the CEO in fewer words. But, since this section articulates the foundation on which all the other sections in this part rest, clarity is worth a bit of redundancy. Just as there are different ways of transferring the football from the quarterback to a running back or receiver, so there are different ways to delegate authority to a CEO. As Section 4.1 makes clear, the board's delegation to the CEO is complete so long as he stays within the lines drawn by the policies in the BPM.

Although some boards engage several staff members to support the board in its governance role, it is best to establish the CEO as the "one agent" of the board. When board members feel unconstrained in requesting information from, giving advice to, or even directing policy toward senior managers other than the CEO, the organization can become dysfunctional. In all likelihood, those senior managers were hired by and report to the CEO, not the board, and the board has no right to try to supervise them or to hold them directly accountable. Even when the board requires that certain senior staff members be approved by the board prior to being hired, the board should then release those people to the supervision of the CEO. Besides, when board members appear to "speak" as a board to more than one person, it can cause competition, mistrust, and confusion among staff members in their day-to-day operations.

We like the explicit permission in Section 4.1.2 for the CEO to "take charge." Between meetings, you want a CEO who makes decisions, tries new ideas, and learns from mistakes. You want the CEO to feel challenged as a professional and not stymied until the board next meets to approve "big decisions." With the BPM, the board, in effect, says, "Go for it. We are giving you considerable leeway. Just don't violate the BPM. And when you disagree with the BPM, we want to hear your recommendations for change." That message is what gets a good CEO up in the morning excited about her job.

Section 4.1.3 reminds everyone that the dynamic between the board and the CEO/staff can change. As the board develops more confidence in management, it may alter the BPM to allow the CEO more discretion in implementing board policy. When the board receives information that causes concern, the board can tighten up its delegated authority by changing the BPM accordingly. Bob likes to say, "When the board and CEO develop a mutual respect for one another's authority and function as partners in defining governance, the dance is fun and the organization will hum."

Finally, in Section 4.1.4, we address a common problem: frequent requests from individual board members that cost unreasonable amounts of staff time and money. Someone has to make the decisions as to whether staff time should be allotted to fulfilling a particular request from a board member. In this situation, the board is saying to the CEO, "We trust you to make that call." Practically, of course, the CEO talks with the chair about denying requests from individual board members. As you will see later in this chapter, there are ways for board members to stay continually informed and therefore reduce their need to request information from the staff.

4.2 CEO Job Description. As the board's single official link to the operating organization, CEO performance will be considered to be synonymous with organizational performance as a whole. Consequently, the CEO's job contributions can be stated as performance in two areas: (a) organizational accomplishment of the major organizational goals in Section 2.8, and (b) organization operations within the boundaries of prudence and ethics established in board policies on Executive Parameters.

We have seen CEO job descriptions that are as short and simple as the one in our BPM template and others that are three pages of bullet points. Often CEO job descriptions are drawn up and closely followed during the recruiting process, but then are seldom consulted after the CEO is hired. Once the CEO is on board, the framework for the CEO/board relationship is less one of listing all the functions in the CEO's job description and more about how well the mission is being accomplished. Accordingly, the board normally looks at the CEO's "job" as being responsible for carrying out the mission of the organization while staying within the stated board policies. As a practical matter, of course, there are many factors that may complicate this simple equation, including the maturity of the organization, external influences, and other factors that are beyond the CEO's control. Accountability must be balanced with fairness as you lay out the relationship between the board and your CEO.

Recall that BPM Section 2.8 lists the current goals of the organization and therefore of the CEO. The board and the CEO mutually agree upon these, and they become the basis of the CEO's evaluation. They should be measurable and linked to the strategic plan. Therefore, even though the board is looking to the CEO to accomplish the mission in a broad sense, it must translate that overarching statement into fair and reasonable goals against which the CEO can be evaluated. We discuss CEO evaluation further under BPM Section 4.5.

4.3 Communication and Counsel to the Board. With respect to providing information and counsel to the board, the CEO shall keep the board informed about matters essential to carrying out its policy duties. Accordingly, the CEO shall:

    4.3.1 Inform the board of relevant trends, anticipated adverse media coverage, and material external and internal changes, particularly changes in the assumptions upon which any board policy has previously been established, always presenting

information in as clear and concise a format as
possible.

4.3.2 Relate to the board as a whole except when fulfilling reasonable individual requests for information or responding to officers or committees
duly charged by the board.

4.3.3 Report immediately any actual or anticipated
material noncompliance with a policy of the
board, along with suggested changes.

The board does not need to know everything that goes on in
an organization, but neither does it want surprises in certain strategic or sensitive areas. In addition to more formal monitoring,
stated in BPM Section 4.4, there will be information that comes to
the attention of the CEO that the board should know about. Good
news tends to be quickly disseminated from the CEO to the board,
but bad news can sometimes take a circuitous route. Yet slow-
traveling bad news often picks up debris on its way to the board,
and CEOs do well to share bad news as promptly as good news.
This open-ended expectation for the CEO is how the CEO helps
board members understand the business that they are in and how
the external world may be affecting their mission.

How specific you make this section is up to you. If you have a
seasoned CEO, whom you trust to convey bad and good news
with equal speed and accuracy, you may be satisfied to make a
general appeal to his good judgment. If you have had a bad experience with a CEO or if he is new on the job, you may be more
prescriptive in this section.

4.4 Monitoring Executive Performance. The purpose of
monitoring is to determine the degree to which the mission
is being accomplished and board policies are being fulfilled. Information that does not do this shall not be considered monitoring. Monitoring will be as automatic as

possible, using a minimum of board time, so that meetings can be used to affect the future rather than to review the past. A given policy may be monitored in one or more of three ways:

4.4.1 *Direct board inspection:* Discovery of compliance information by a board member, a committee, or the board as a whole. This includes board inspection of documents, activities, or circumstances that allows a "prudent person" test of policy compliance.

4.4.2 *External report:* Discovery of compliance information by a disinterested, external person or firm who is selected by and reports directly to the board. Such reports must assess executive performance only against legal requirements or policies of the board, with suggestions from the external party as to how the organization can improve itself.

4.4.3 *CEO reports:* The CEO shall help the board determine what tracking data are available to measure progress in achieving the mission and goals and conforming with board policies. Currently the board requests these regular monitoring reports, in addition to any specific reports requested in other sections of the BPM:

4.4.3.1 Monthly: Informal CEO reports on achievements, problems, and board notices.

4.4.3.2 Quarterly: (a) A one- or two-page "dashboard" report showing agreed-upon key indicators that track designated financial and program results over a three-year period in graphic form; (b) other summary reports as the board may define in this BPM.

4.4.3.3 Semiannually: (a) Expense and revenue against budget report with comparison to previous year; (b) balance sheet; (c) cash flow projections; (d) membership statistics.

4.4.3.4 Annually: Within 45 days of the end of the fiscal year, (a) end-of-year expense and revenue against budget; (b) balance sheet; (c) staff organization chart (or whenever major changes are made); (d) other reports that the board may define in this BPM.

Recall the principles that we have established so far, that board policy is:

1. Formulated by board members and the CEO
2. Set by the full board
3. Implemented by the CEO
4. Monitored by the board

We have found that most boards fall down on the last step. This BPM section describes a policy that is designed to deal with some of the shortcomings in boards' approaches to monitoring.

Section 4.4 lists the three sources of information/data that the board will use to monitor progress on its policies. The first (Section 4.4.1, direct board inspection) is included because everything that a board member sees and hears eventually forms an impression in his mind that may be difficult to offset or clarify without supplemental data. That is why there need to be other sources of data for board monitoring. The second source (Section 4.4.2, external reports) refers primarily to the reports by your financial auditors, although certain sectors may require semiofficial external reviews, e.g., by accrediting bodies, science grant peer review panels, OSHA inspectors, and other such agencies. The board should not overlook the possibility of commissioning voluntary external assessments of a program area or operational unit such as HR, although most CEOs are astute enough to pay attention to those areas when they pick up board concerns. The third source of information (Section 4.3.3, CEO reports) is where the board and the CEO need to communicate clearly. Most boards simply get copies of management reports, which are often too detailed, too long, and too confusing. The board needs to be clear about what it wants and in what format. This information sheds light on the CEO's job performance, but its primary function is to measure results against mission.

Monitoring is an art and a science that the majority of nonprofits have yet to master. In our board workshops, we use the Good Nonprofit Board Reports handout like the downloadable document listed in Appendix B to help boards think through the form, content, and frequency of their internal reports. It is a summary of the features of reports to the board that we have found effective for the CEO in communicating with the board.

4.5 Annual Performance Review. A performance evaluation task force, comprising the board chair, the vice chair, and the chair of the Governance Committee, shall formally evaluate the CEO annually, based on achievement of organizational goals and any other specific goals that the board and the CEO have agreed upon in advance, as well as the CEO's own written self-evaluation and invited comments from all board members after they have seen the self-evaluation. The chair shall serve as chair of the task force. After meeting with the CEO, the task force will report on its review to the board, including recommendations on the CEO's compensation, which the Executive Committee or the board will then act upon.

During this process, the CEO and the board will agree on any specific, personal performance goals for the year ahead. These goals shall be documented in a letter to the CEO from the board chair and will be a primary basis for determining the CEO's performance at the end of the next year. At least every three years, the task force shall invite other input in a carefully planned "360" review, inviting feedback from staff, peers in our sector, and individuals outside the organization who have interacted with the CEO.

Performance reviews are tough enough when one has a single boss, but when the "boss" comprises multiple personalities, performance reviews are especially complicated. Of all the functions that a board is responsible for, perhaps none is so often discounted or neglected outright as the CEO annual performance review. This unhappy occurrence can result from a lack of clarity concerning the process or from a failure to carry out the process in the manner prescribed by the board. BPM Section 4.5 is intended to eliminate the first reason for a board's failure to conduct a fair evaluation of the CEO. It describes a straightforward annual evaluation process that includes the configuration of the task force conducting the review, the input from the board, the role of the CEO's self-evaluation, and the ultimate approval of the board.

You may want to include more detail in this section, such as a more specific timetable for the evaluation or more specifics on the basis for evaluation. Often boards will tie the completion date to a meeting, e.g., the first meeting after the end of the fiscal year, or to the completion of the annual audit.

The composition of the performance review group (a task force in the template) is an important ingredient in the process. We prefer that at least three key board members be involved, and normally the chair plays the most prominent role in the process. However, give some thought to this issue before you automatically appoint your board chair as the chair of your task force. Someone other than the chair may be more objective and more constructively critical of the CEO. The composition and leadership of the task force should be up to the board, and may change from time to time.

The credibility of the evaluation is also highly dependent on the process that the task force employs. Notice that the task force is required to invite input from the other board members after everyone has read the CEO's written self-evaluation. Ideally, the task force will guide the CEO in what she might provide in that self-evaluation. As a general rule, the five- to eight-page document should include progress on both organizational goals and personal goals agreed upon the year before by the CEO and the evaluation task force. Often, board members have good insight into a CEO's talents and strengths and can merge those with their perceptions of organizational needs. No CEO can be strong in everything. Here is a chance to focus the CEO's time and energy to produce the best results.

There are a number of "score sheets" out there for you to consider. Note that we suggest using a "360" evaluation process at least every three years. These types of evaluations can be very informative and helpful to the CEO, but if they are poorly handled, they can do more harm than good. Our Section 4.5 states that the 360 evaluation must be "carefully planned." With some organizations, we have been more specific, requiring that the board hire an experienced consultant to initiate the process and possibly to supervise its implementation for the first two or three cycles. If you are uncertain about your board's ability to carry out an objective, constructive 360 evaluation of your CEO, invest in a professional consultant who uses a proven process or leave this evaluation out of your BPM.

Whatever the process you use for evaluating your CEO, involve your CEO as a true partner in its development. The purpose of evaluation is more for affirmation and focusing on the future than for unnecessary criticism. When CEOs are comfortable with the process, most of them actually welcome this annual event, as they need and desire honest feedback. Good CEOs will be surprisingly candid and accurate in their self-evaluation, although they often rate themselves too harshly. That being said, in 10 to 15 percent of cases (our best guess), the annual evaluation process triggers a serious discussion as to whether the CEO is still the best fit for the job, leading to a voluntary or forced resignation. But that's worth a separate book.

4.6 Staff Compensation. The CEO is expected to hire, train, motivate, compensate, and terminate staff in a professional and caring fashion. Salaries will be set at between X% and Y% of the mean for salaries in organizations of similar size, budget, and location. Benefits will include. . . . The CEO shall (a) develop and maintain an employee manual that is reviewed annually by competent legal counsel and (b) provide copies of this manual to the board for information around April 1 of each year.

This section is fairly short compared to the importance of staff members in terms of their contributions and their cost. We believe that most personnel issues are in the management realm, but the board surely has something to say about human resources. First, in general terms, it wants the CEO to take all aspects of the personnel function seriously. Some boards will go so far as to review and approve the salaries of some or all staff members. While we do not favor the board's being involved at that level of detail, there may be a principle or a strategic issue related to the staff compensation. Specifically, we believe that the board should state its philosophy about compensation. Do you want to be the highest-paying organization in your city? Or the lowest? It is reasonable to state a range that, when applied to commonly available compensation surveys, will guide the CEO in setting compensation for positions similar to those in the salary surveys. We do not get into which other benefits an organization should offer, but we do believe that the board should state its minimums. Surely the board should set the amount of the organization's contribution to a pension program. And given the high cost of health insurance, something in this section about sharing of premiums might be important.

This section is a good place to remind you of one of our fundamental distinctions between the one voice of the board (BPM) and many other written policies that are more properly owned by the CEO. In this case, the board asks to *see* the personnel manual. When board members see it, they may be tempted to vote to approve it, but that would make it a board document. Or someone on the board might make a motion to change a paragraph in the personnel manual. Oops again! The board must stick to its own document (the BPM) by changing what it wants to change in Section 4.6, then expecting the CEO to rewrite the personnel manual immediately to comply with the BPM. For example, if the CEO had put in the personnel manual a full tuition policy for any staff member pursuing education, and the board thought that this was too extravagant for the organization's financial condition, the board might insert in Section 4.6 this short sentence: "Any tuition reimbursement plan shall require an employee first to work full time for at least one year before receiving 50 percent reimbursement of actual tuition paid."

We hope this principle is catching on!

> ***4.7 Staff Treatment.*** With respect to treatment of paid and volunteer staff, the CEO may not cause or allow conditions that are inhumane, unfair, or undignified. Accordingly, he may not:
>
> 4.7.1 Discriminate among employees on other than clearly job-related, individual performance or qualifications.
>
> 4.7.2 Fail to take reasonable steps to protect staff from unsafe or unhealthy conditions.
>
> 4.7.3 Withhold from staff a due-process, unbiased grievance procedure.
>
> 4.7.4 Discriminate against any staff member for expressing an ethical dissent.
>
> 4.7.5 Prevent staff from grieving to the board when (a) internal grievance procedures have been exhausted and (b) the employee alleges that board policy has been violated to his or her detriment.
>
> 4.7.6 Fail to acquaint staff members with their rights under this policy.

We include this rather specific section in our template because too many nonprofit boards are not as sensitive to these issues as are many staff members—and the courts. Whether because of explicit legal requirements or because they are just good practices, we want to encourage boards to insist that these basic practices be enforced. We realize that this Section 4.7 could be multiple pages in length, but we prefer to trust the CEO to put fuller explanations of employee roles, rights, and responsibilities in the personnel manual.

4.8 CEO Transitions. At any time, the chair may appoint a transition task force to explore options and propose strategies and board policies related to succession and transition of the CEO and to facilitate any special needs of the outgoing and incoming CEOs and their families. The incumbent CEO shall give the board, if possible, a(n) _____ month notice of intent to leave that office. Any need for an acting or interim CEO will be determined by the board chair subject to board approval. The board chair is authorized, as soon as a vacancy or scheduled departure of the CEO is known, to appoint a search committee and committee chair. The search committee may include up to two people not on the board. The committee shall within 30 days recommend for board approval a position announcement, a recommendation on any search consultant, the appointment of a search secretary, and a budget for the search. The search committee shall present one or two qualified candidates to the full board for selection. A special task force appointed by the chair shall, at the time of selection, negotiate the new CEO's compensation and service agreement and give both the incumbent and the successor CEO any special performance priorities from the board. After he/she leaves the organization, the outgoing CEO may be given a paid role, but only with the approval of the new CEO in consultation with the officers and the board.

Few events can be as disruptive to an organization as the departure of the CEO. Yet in our experience, not enough organizations have a plan of action in case their CEO dies suddenly or leaves after giving insufficient notice. BPM Section 4.8 outlines some of the features of a transition plan that may go into a BPM. It describes who has the authority to do what during the transition period. You may also decide to develop a more detailed succession planning document, in which case your BPM would incorporate that document by reference. We include among the downloadable material listed in Appendix B a checklist of items that you will probably want to cover in your transition or your succession plan.

> **4.9** *Board Reference Book and Web Site.* In addition to reports that the CEO may choose to make to the board, the CEO shall develop and maintain a Board Reference Book with all pertinent documents to which board members might want to refer during board and committee meetings (e.g., articles, bylaws, organization chart, recent minutes, committee roster, list of key volunteers/consultants, board documents referred to in this BPM, etc.). In addition, the board requests that the CEO maintain, as funding is available, a secure Internet web site for board members to allow them to access relevant data and reports on a timely basis. The CEO shall notify board members as new key information is posted to the board web site.

Because it has to do with the board–CEO/staff relationship, we finish Part 4 with a requirement that board-related documents be made available to board members when they need them. Since we discuss the Board Reference Book in Chapter 11 of this book, we will mention here only that the Board Reference Book is a valuable supplement to the BPM. Board members must be educated and at least be made aware of a number of other documents that will inform board action. With respect to the Internet, more and more organizations are using it to communicate with their board members, both using e-mails and using confidential (and even public) sections of their web sites. In fact, because of the efficiency of using the Internet, we expect that some organizations will even use "access to the Internet" as a desirable if not necessary requirement for board membership.

✧

So far, the BPM has addressed the organizational essentials, the board's own structure and process, and, in this chapter, policies relating to the board's important relationship with its CEO and its staff. There is just one more open-ended topic that the BPM must address: the parameters that the board feels are necessary to put around the CEO's administrative duties. You are well down the road to a completed journey!

CHAPTER 10

BPM Part 5: Executive Parameters

Authority without wisdom is like a heavy ax without an edge, fitter to bruise than to polish.

—Anne Bradstreet

One of the criticisms of the Policy Governance model (and by association any model that rests on a policy manual like the BPM) is that its power is concentrated in the hands of a few people (the board) and that the staff may feel that the board is disconnected because board members see themselves more in a governing role than in a operating role.[1] We don't doubt that boards that operate from a policy perspective may appear to the staff to be distant, nor do we question the natural tension that arises when one person or group tells another what that person or group can or cannot do. However, we don't see this as being as much a problem with policy manuals as it is a problem with the attitude of the board and how it documents and communicates its policies. That the board has the authority is stipulated. How the board uses the authority is the real issue. Exercising authority without wisdom will doom any governance model.

Part 5 of the BPM contains those specific policies that the board wants to apply to the various operating functions within the organization. For a board that is more "hands on," this may be the longest part of the BPM. For a board that is more relaxed in its prescriptions, Part 5 may be only a few pages. Our template is probably in the low-average range.

We include four main sections of Part 5, each corresponding to one of the functional committees shown in BPM Part 3 (Chapter 8): finance, programs, advancement, and audit and compliance. As with the number of committees that you establish, we have no fixed view on the number of sections in this part. You can always separate those that seem to warrant it and consolidate others. For example, we have shown investment policies in Section 5.2, "Finance Parameters", but some organizations prefer to separate these functions. Some organizations will have separate sections for communications and fund-raising, although because we see considerable overlap in these two functions, we like to combine them under "Advancement Parameters." Many smaller boards will include their audit and compliance policies in the finance section (Section 5.2 in the template). Some boards that have a particular concern about liability or related issues may use an entire section in Part 5 for risk management policies.

The number of section headings and the number of policies under each heading in Part 5 varies with the size and type of the organization, the size of the staff, and other factors such as the maturity of the organization and the clarity and coverage of the CEO's operating procedures. What we have included in the template are sample policies only. Although these policies are taken from actual BPMs, in the template they are meant to be for illustrative purposes only.

5.1 General Guidance. The purpose of the remainder of the BPM is to detail those executive parameters that will guide the CEO and the staff as they accomplish the mission. These parameters are intended to free the CEO and the staff to make timely decisions without undue board directives. The board expects that the CEO will do nothing that is illegal, unethical, or imprudent. Beyond these general parameters, the board details its executive parameters in the major sections that follow in Part 5.

Before this BPM Part 5 addresses the individual functions of the organization, it offers this general statement of the purpose of the executive parameters (Part 5) and some overarching advice as to what the board expects from its CEO. The input for the policies in this part can emanate from the board, the CEO, or the staff as these parties seek to fulfill their respective roles in the organization. Accordingly, while the policies in Part 5 are written in a manner that guides or limits the CEO and the staff, they are intended to benefit all parties in that they clarify roles and expectations. The parameters (or limitations, as they may be called) offer bright lines within which the CEO and staff are free to operate.

5.2 Finance Parameters. The CEO must ensure that the financial integrity of the organization is maintained at all times; that proper care is exercised in the receiving, processing, and disbursing of funds; and that financial and non-financial assets are appropriately protected.

As indicated in the introduction to Part 5, Section 5.2 can cover one, some, or all of the common financial subjects, e.g., budgeting, financial controls, investments, and auditing. For purposes of the template, we have chosen to include the first three functions and to put auditing with compliance.

5.2.1 Budgeting. The budget during any fiscal period shall not (a) deviate materially from the board's goals and priorities listed in Part 2, (b) risk fiscal jeopardy, or (c) fail to show a generally acceptable level of foresight. Accordingly, the CEO may not cause or allow budgeting that:

5.2.1.1 Contains too little detail to (a) enable accurate projection of revenues and expenses, (b) separate capital items from operational items, (c) monitor cash flow and subsequent audit trails, and (d) disclose planning assumptions.

5.2.1.2 Anticipates the expenditure in any fiscal year of more funds than are conservatively projected to be received in that period.

5.2.1.3 Reduces the current assets at any time to less than twice current liabilities or allows cash to drop below a safety reserve of $_____ at any time.

5.2.1.4 Provides less than $_____ for board prerogatives during the year, such as costs of the annual audit and board development.

5.2.1.5 Is not derived from the strategic plan.

Few documents receive more scrutiny from the board than the annual budget. In fact, some boards feel that approving the budget and measuring the organization by how well it stays within the budget are 95 percent of their job. While we see this as a clearly short-sighted view of the board's overall responsibility, we agree that the annual budget is one area where the board needs to make its expectations plain and in writing. This does not mean that we recommend that the board prepare the budget, any more than we recommend that the board be the primary author of the strategic plan. The CEO and the staff are normally in the best position to draft the strategic plan and annual budget and present them to the board for its review. If the board has some principles that it expects to be observed in the process, this section is the place to document them.

Some boards see budgeting as being more appropriately combined with planning and will therefore have a section entitled

"Planning and Budgeting." More typically, however, the members of the finance committee will tend to have the skill sets to work with budget data, and they are likely to be the people you expect to conduct more detailed analyses of budget variances and other financial reviews. Besides, we are not keen on the board's listing "planning" as one of its primary functions because it suggests too strong a role for the board in what we believe should be a CEO-initiated function.

> *5.2.2 Financial Controls.* The CEO must exercise care in accounting for and protecting the financial assets of the organization. To this end, the CEO is expected to incorporate generally accepted accounting principles and internal controls in the financial systems that are employed in the organization. In addition, the CEO may not:
> 5.2.2.1 Receive, process, or disburse funds under controls insufficient to meet the board-appointed auditor's standards.
> 5.2.2.2 Approve an unbudgeted expenditure or commitment of greater than $_____ without the approval of the full board.
> 5.2.2.3 Approve an unbudgeted expenditure or commitment of greater than $_____ without the approval of the Finance Committee.

Section 5.2.2.1 shows this board effectively deferring to its auditor in setting standards for financial controls. If you have a good process for hiring and working with a reputable auditor each year, this is usually an efficient way for the board to communicate its policy. If you want to be more specific about matters like accounting treatments, separation of duties, and the like, your auditor can probably give you a good checklist, or you will find plenty of information on the Internet by searching on "financial controls."

Most boards will use the budget to apply financial controls for expenditures that are anticipated in the budget. For unanticipated or unbudgeted items, in Sections 5.2.2.2 and 5.2.2.3, the board is giving the CEO the dollar limits of her approval authority before she needs the approval of the full board or the finance committee. How much approval authority you give your CEO is another variable that will depend on the size of your budget, your comfort with the CEO, the typical types of purchases, the detail in your budget, and the lead times involved in the transaction. Another approach to this policy is simply to require that the CEO notify the board or the finance committee, rather than requiring board or committee approval. This technique avoids surprises at the board level, but is also more efficient for the CEO. Work with your CEO to decide on the appropriate dollar amounts and the desirable type of notification or approval process, write the policy into the BPM, and change it over time as necessary.

5.2.3 Asset Protection. The CEO may not allow assets to be unprotected, inadequately maintained, or unnecessarily risked. Accordingly, the CEO may not:

5.2.3.1 Fail to insure against theft and casualty losses to at least 80 percent of replacement cost and against liability losses to board members, staff, or the organization itself beyond the minimally acceptable prudent level.

5.2.3.2 Allow nonbonded personnel access to material amounts of funds.

5.2.3.3 Subject office equipment to improper wear and tear or insufficient maintenance.

5.2.3.4 Unnecessarily expose the organization, its board, or its staff to claims of liability.

5.2.3.5 Make any major purchase of over $_____ without sealed bids or some other demonstrably prudent method of acquisition of quality goods, or any purchase of over $_____ without a written record of competitive prices, or

> any purchase wherein normally prudent protection against conflict of interest has not been provided.
> 5.2.3.6 Acquire, encumber, or dispose of real property without board approval.

This section could also be labeled more generally as "Risk Management." The policies shown in Sections 5.2.3.1 through 5.2.3.6 are common expressions from the board as to how it wants the CEO to protect the nonfinancial assets of the organization. Notice that in Section 5.2.3.1, the board is specific about the level of insurance, i.e., that it be no lower than 80 percent of replacement cost. You may want to add detail here, such as which items must be insured at replacement cost and which items may be covered at a lower amount.

Each of the sample policies shown in these sections is subject to expansion to include specific dollar amounts or degrees of protection. Finally, there is no requirement to include any of these policies if you are confident that they fall under the general charges to the CEO in Sections 5.1 and 5.2.

> *5.2.4 Investment Principles.* The CEO may not invest or hold operating capital in insecure instruments, including uninsured checking accounts and bonds of less than AA rating, or in non-interest-bearing accounts, except where necessary to facilitate operational transactions.

Most nonprofits don't have the luxury of large endowments, and their boards may not perceive the need to prescribe the investment options that the CEO must operate within. However, even cash-strapped organizations shouldn't overlook the value of simple guidance in this area. For example, Section 5.2.4 gives what amounts to a "bare bones" outline on how the organization's cash should be maintained. Some boards will have one set of parameters for how short-term capital may be invested and another set of parameters for long-term capital. Boards with multiple endowments or funds may even have a separate policy for each fund.

Obviously, as the amounts available for investment increase, so does the obligation of the board to communicate its policies on investments to the CEO. Unless your CEO has expertise in this area, he will probably welcome the board's guidance here. Too many real or perceived scandals in the nonprofit sector arise from the misuse of investment funds. While you don't want to tie the CEO's hands, you do want to document specific enough policies to ensure that the lines are clearly drawn and consistently honored.

5.3 Program Parameters. In general, the CEO is expected to establish, maintain, and eliminate programs and services to achieve the organization's mission and goals in the most effective and efficient manner.

  5.3.1 New programs should be projected to serve at least _____ people.

  5.3.2 New programs with an expected budget exceeding $_____ must be approved by the board. Those programs now approved include:

  5.3.3 Programs with costs of more than $_____ shall be assessed for effectiveness by an outside evaluator at least every three years, with a written report being made available to the board.

  5.3.4 Any program executed in partnership with another organization shall _____.

This is another section that will vary greatly among nonprofit organizations. Many nonprofits have a simple mission that is carried out through one or two programs. Others will have broad missions that are being served by a wide range of programs, some of them ongoing and others time-limited and constantly changing. As with any other BPM section, the board's perspective vis-à-vis its organization's programs is at a strategic level. For example, in Section 5.3, the board is explaining to the CEO that it looks to her to form programs, decide whether they are working, and modify or eliminate them as appropriate. However, as detail to the broad authority given in Section 5.3, the board goes on to say in Sections 5.3.1 through 5.3.4 that it has certain criteria that must be met before a program can be implemented, e.g., the program must:

- Serve a threshold number of people (Section 5.3.1)
- Receive board approval if it is over a threshold dollar amount (Section 5.3.2)
- Receive a special review if costs exceed a certain amount (Section 5.3.3)
- Meet certain requirements if it involves partnering with another organization (Section 5.3.4)

We have also seen policies that limit the amount of subsidy that a program may receive without board approval or that require a new program to pay for itself within a certain period after implementation. The board may also tie these policies to the strategic plan by allowing the CEO a free hand with programs that are documented in the strategic plan, but requiring that certain criteria be met for programs that are not specifically mentioned in the strategic plan.

5.4 Advancement Parameters. The various efforts to represent the organization to the public (media, public relations, fund-raising, new member recruitment, etc.) shall be integrated sufficiently so that the organization's brand/positioning in the external world is positive and effective.

    5.4.1 *Fund-Raising Strategy.* The CEO shall develop and maintain a fund-raising plan that, at a minimum, includes direct mail, major donor initiatives, planned giving, and Web-based giving. Such plan shall be provided to board members for review each March, along with results for each initiative. Total direct and indirect expenses for fund-raising shall not exceed 22 percent of the total budget.

5.4.1.1 *Donor Bill of Rights.* The CEO shall develop a Donor Bill of Rights and provide the latest version to the board; this shall include, *inter alia*, the following restrictions: the CEO may not allow the names of donors to be revealed outside the organization, represent to a donor that an action will be taken that violates board policies, fail to honor a request from a donor as to how her/his contribution is to be allocated, fail to confirm receipt of a donor's contribution, or fail to send a donor an annual summary of donations.

5.4.1.2 *Training.* The CEO shall ensure that appropriate members of the board and staff receive annual training in new fund-raising techniques and shall budget for such expenses.

For reasons that we explain in Chapter 8, we prefer the label "advancement" for the activities of fund-raising, development, communications, public relations, marketing, and branding. We have found considerable overlap in these functional areas, and believe that attempts to compartmentalize policies by the individual areas are difficult because of the arbitrary distinctions that are often required.

With respect to fund-raising, most organizations and boards put donor satisfaction at the top of their priority list. The profile of your donors will say a lot about how you set policies for their care and feeding. If you have a membership organization with a fairly broad, homogeneous donor population, a small number of general policies such as those in Section 5.4 may be sufficient. However, if you have a mixed profile—such as several large donors, some corporate sponsors, and a few thousand small do-nors—chances are that you will have an individual fund-raising strategy for each segment of your profile. Methods for contacting donors will range from individual visits to mass mailings, and rules for who may contact which donor segments will also vary across the profile.

But having different rules for different donor types does not mean that the board must dictate how the CEO and the staff should go about their fund-raising duties. The board can simply identify the boundaries within which the CEO must stay and let him develop the individual donor relations strategies within those limits. If your board has an aversion to a particular type of fund-raising, e.g., telephone soliciting, put that prohibition into the BPM. You also may want to require that contact with certain top donors be made only by the CEO or a board member. If so, put the restriction in here.

We have found that on many, if not on most, nonprofit boards, there is an expectation that board members will assist with fund-raising. The problem is that this expectation is not always clearly documented. If you expect your board members to be fund-raisers, let them know this ahead of time. Put this in Part 3, where you lay out the expectations for board members (Sections 3.1 through 3.3). Also put it in the board profile (Appendix C). However, be careful how you identify the fund-raising requirements. For example, if you want "good fund-raiser" to be listed on the profile, put it in as a desirable trait, not a mandatory one. Finding good people for your board may become considerably more difficult if the candidates have to satisfy requirements vis-à-vis diversity, skills, and experience and then be good fund-raisers as well.

Besides, fund-raising means different things to different peo-ple. Some board members are happy to take a large donor out to lunch and talk about her golf game or her family vacations, with an occasional good word thrown in about the value of the donor's investment in the organization. But that same member may be to-tally resistant to making a few phone calls to friends to ask them to support a capital campaign for the organization. Therefore, if you want a policy that requires board members to assist in fund-raising commensurate with their individual skills and personalities, be flexible about just how the board member can help. This may mean that a couple of your more introverted board members are stuffing envelopes rather than making telephone calls, but then, they may be the very people that you need on a critical committee or task force.

5.4.2 Public Affairs. The CEO shall exercise care in representing that we are a charitable, mission-centered, listening organization and shall develop policies and procedures for communicating with primary stakeholders and the public at large in a way that reinforces that image.

    5.4.2.1 **Communications Plan.** The CEO shall develop and maintain a communications plan, shared with the board as appropriate, that describes how the organization will communicate with its various stakeholders. The plan shall identify the stakeholder segments, how the organization will both speak and listen to each segment, and who is allowed to speak for the organization. The plan shall also include the role of board members both as "listeners" and as "speakers" for the organization.

    5.4.2.2 **Communication Restrictions.** To preserve our image in the community, the CEO and any designee are the only spokespersons authorized to speak for the organization, and the chair is the only spokesperson for the board. None of the spokespersons may represent the organization in any way that is inconsistent with the policies in Part 2 of this BPM; make statements that may be perceived as supporting a political party or platform; be the author of an article, book, or publication that includes classified or sensitive information about

> the organization; or engage in lobbying activi-
> ties at any governmental level without prior
> permission from the board.

Nonprofit organizations, like their for-profit counterparts, have brands in the marketplace. Their reputation in the public square plays no small role in their success or failure. Protecting the brand is one of the primary purposes of a communications strategy, and every organization is wise to make this a material part of its strategic plan.

Policies dealing with communications may be viewed by the CEO and the staff as gags on their free speech. For example, they may perceive Section 5.4.2.2 as being too wide-ranging and prone to abuse by the board. They may feel that if this section is interpreted too strictly, even a mild criticism of the organization uttered by a staff person at a public meeting could be viewed as a cause for rebuke or discipline. They may reason that, after all, you cannot police every conversation that the staff has.

We agree that general policy statements such as Section 5.4.2.2 could be used to punish a CEO or staff member for a simple remark in public, but there is another side to that coin. We are reminded of the aphorism, "A man is master of his words until they are spoken; after that, the reverse is true," which applies to organizations as well as to individuals. Too many organizations, nonprofit and for-profit, are sent scrambling to their public relations consultants after a board member, CEO, or staff member makes an ill-advised comment or criticism in public. Although having a policy that covers these situations is no guarantee that they won't happen, it can communicate the board's expectation that everyone in the organization is responsible for the culture of the organization and the image that the organization projects to its immediate community and the public at large. Failure to meet that responsibility sends the message that the individual is more concerned about himself than about the organization, a point that conflicts with another corporate value: teamwork.

5.5 Audit and Compliance Parameters. The CEO shall take the necessary steps to ensure the integrity of our systems and procedures; to see that they comply with all pertinent legal, regulatory, and professional requirements; and to report to the board any material variations or violations.

> 5.5.1 *Annual External Audit.* An independent auditor will be hired and supervised by the Audit and Compliance Committee, after a careful selection and annual evaluation. The CEO shall work with the auditor to gain a clean opinion on the annual financial statements and respond in detail to items in the auditor's management letter concerning opportunities to improve systems and procedures related to financial controls.

> 5.5.2 *Internal Compliance.* The CEO shall meet all requirements for complying with federal, state, or local laws and regulations. The CEO shall maintain a list of compliance actions and reports that are required of a nonprofit organization and periodically submit the list for inspection by the Audit and Compliance Committee. On a biennial basis, starting in FY____, the CEO shall contract for a legal review of the organization's compliance with the pertinent laws and regulations and make the results of the review available to the Audit and Compliance Committee, which, in turn, will report to the board on the overall status of the organization with respect to compliance matters, including any current problems or anticipated problems with regulatory authorities.

The substantive portion of Section 5.5 draws heavily on the organization's interaction with the board-appointed auditor and on the sundry laws and regulations that affect the organization. Several states require nonprofits that are over a threshold size to have an audit conducted by an independent auditor using generally accepted auditing standards. The federal government and most of the states have annual reporting requirements as well. The gist of Section 5.5 is to communicate to the CEO the expectation that she is responsible for meeting all of these requirements and for giving the board access to information that will show that these requirements are being satisfied.

The requirement for a legal review (Section 5.5.2) may appear to be "belt and suspenders," but some boards want that extra measure of comfort in the compliance area. Some boards are content to give the CEO a broad statement such as that in Section 5.5, while others prefer an even more stringent policy of requiring a legal audit on an annual (rather than a biennial) basis.

> **5.6 Miscellaneous.** [Include other policies that don't naturally fit into one of the other major sections.]

Each nonprofit is unique in some ways. Your board may want to give your CEO additional "parameters" in an area that does not fit naturally into the main sections that we suggest in our template. Those board policies would go in this Section 5.6.

Working with Part 5

Of the parts in the BPM, Part 5 probably gets the most attention after the board has been operating with the BPM for a while. Once the administrative issues have been established in Part 1, the strategic direction set in Part 2, the governance model defined in Part 3, and the board–CEO/staff relationships outlined in Part 4, there remains the job of "working at the board–CEO boundaries" in Part 5. These boundaries or parameters will rarely remain constant, as new information and new situations will inform the thinking of either the board or the CEO. Policies in the form of guidance to or limitations on the CEO will come and go, but mostly they will be refined. Threshold amounts will be changed, reporting deadlines adjusted, program criteria changed, or communications rules modified.

All this changing of policies may suggest an unstable or disorganized board. In fact, it's just the opposite. Active and innovative CEOs and responsive boards are constantly looking for ways to do their jobs better, and they gain comfort from an openness to new ideas and from knowing that if a policy isn't working, it can be changed at the next board meeting. Perhaps you have been on boards that are reluctant to develop a particular written policy for fear that it will fail to have the desired effect or, worse, have a negative effect. They end up with "analysis paralysis," as they continue to study the issue and never make a decision. The result of forgoing a written policy is to bump along with the implicit policy, which is almost always followed unevenly, rather than documenting the policy and adjusting it as dictated by the results. But avoiding this mode of board operations is what the third leg of the roadmap is all about.

✧

You now have completed the second leg of your journey. It took some work, but you will soon begin enjoying the fruits of those labors as you exercise your BPM. Remember, however, that although you have finished the second leg of the roadmap, you are not finished with the BPM. Far from it. The BPM is your "governance management system." You build a system to use it, not to lose it—and that brings us to Chapter 11.

Are We There Yet? The End of the Beginning

This is not the end. It is not even the beginning of the end. But it is, perhaps, the end of the beginning.

—Winston Churchill, November 10, 1942

Few leaders in history have been as effective as Prime Minister Churchill in rallying their country behind a war effort. In November 1942, the British had just been driven off the European mainland by a superior German force. Had it not been for an enormous effort by a civilian armada of British ships and small boats at Dunkirk, the defeat would have been devastating. Instead, combining his mastery of words with an indefatigable fighting spirit, Churchill declared the defeat to be simply a prologue to the next chapter—indeed, to the beginning of a story of ultimate victory.

We have no illusions about comparing the miracle at Dunkirk with the effort that you have just expended in developing your BPM. Events in policy manual making rarely make the history books. Still, when we discuss our roadmap, we like the Churchillian phrase "the end of the beginning." It marks the completion of one task (a leg of the roadmap), even as it highlights the commencement of another. For all the emphasis on its beginning, however, the irony of this third and last leg of the roadmap is that it has no end.

Once you have developed your initial BPM, albeit at a high level, you embark on the third leg of the roadmap. Every board action thereafter is taken in the context of the BPM, either from the standpoint of following the policies that have already been recorded in the BPM or from the standpoint of formulating policies and approving them for inclusion in the BPM. Every study, discussion, and action is related to either an existing board policy or a prospective board policy. If it's something else, you might question why it is taking the board's time.

Integrating the BPM—Use It or Lose It

The Board Member's Playbook (Playbook)[1] was published in 2004 with the purpose of illustrating to organizations that had implemented the Policy Governance model how to use board policies to "solve problems, make decisions, and build a stronger board."[2] Its 270 notebook-sized pages are published with a soft cover. As a result, it projects the no-nonsense image of a self-help manual, which is its primary purpose. In the foreword to the Playbook, John Carver lays out the rationale behind its publication:

> Real leaders get in front of the parade, and that requires a systematic approach capable of embracing events rather than being driven by them. There is merit knowing that when dilemmas do arise, there is an organized, carefully considered, values-based way not only to solve them but also to move beyond them. Maintaining such exemplary leadership requires *practice*.[3]

The emphasis on the word *practice* is Carver's, although the weight that he gives the word hardly seems necessary. That his wife, Miriam, herself a expert in Policy Governance, and her coauthor, Bill Charney, would devote a book of this size to the subject of practicing the use of a policy manual ought to underscore the need for what we have called the third leg of the roadmap—the integration of the BPM into the governance process. Carver goes on in the foreword:

> And the need [for practice] is even more pronounced in the case of group performance, for interpersonal interaction is added to—or rather becomes an integral and complicated part of—basic skill development. The surprising thing is not that there now is a book on governance rehearsals but that the idea strikes us as novel. That fact is truly a diagnostic comment on the widespread lack of rigor usually brought to the board task.[4]

The fact that the *Playbook* was published more than ten years after the Policy Governance model was being adopted by scores of organizations is testimony enough to the need to highlight the third leg of the roadmap. For we also have seen too many organizations go through the process of developing the BPM, only to use it sparingly in solving board problems and informing board decisions. We hope that it will not be necessary to devote an entire book to practice problems for the BPM, but we do not discount the emphasis on rehearsing decisions using the BPM. As with learning a new language, its use builds confidence, which encourages more use, which adds to the comfort level, which facilitates more use, and so on. To press the analogy further, the most efficient way to learn a new language is typically to immerse yourself in it and in the culture in which it is used.

The same is true with integrating the BPM. Once you have the first version of your BPM, you want it to be your basis of operation, i.e., you want your board to immerse itself in the BPM. From the outset, your BPM should be the voice of the board—the *only* voice of the board. You may have several statements that were policies before you adopted the BPM, but that you have not included in the early versions of the BPM. These former policies may in fact be queued up to be incorporated into your BPM, but they are no longer policies. They are "policies-in-waiting." If you cannot agree on how a policy ought to be written into the BPM, it probably doesn't enjoy the level of board support that every policy should have. It can therefore afford to wait until the board can agree on the BPM language.

In this chapter, we offer some techniques that we believe will allow your BPM to gain traction in your governance structure and processes. These techniques follow logically from the language in the BPM in our template. If you have retained much of the material in our template, therefore, we are in this chapter merely encouraging you to systematically honor the principles and practices in your BPM.

Integrating the BPM: Gaining Traction

To help your BPM get that critical foothold in your board processes, here are a few areas where it can be employed as soon as the first version is approved.

Let It Inform Your Meeting Agenda

One of the first ways in which the BPM can serve your board is by informing your meeting agendas. For example, the CEO's report typically occupies a central place on the board agenda. If you have adopted a set of current goals that your CEO and your board have agreed upon and put into BPM Part 2, those goals should form the basis for the CEO's report to the board at each meeting. For boards that meet frequently, this may mean that the CEO simply reports that there has been no progress on a particular goal or goals. But far from being tedious, this process keeps the list of goals in front of both the CEO and the board and reminds them of the central role that the list plays in maintaining a common CEO/board focus, to say nothing of its being the basis for the CEO's evaluation. Besides, an organization's goals may have been altered throughout the year. The CEO should be encouraged to modify the goals whenever circumstances arise that justify the change. On the one hand, of course, the CEO should not be allowed to adjust a goal simply because he is failing to achieve it.

On the other hand, external factors that affect the assumptions on which a goal was based should lead to its adjustment. A slavish adherence to outdated goals is both unfair to the CEO and unhealthy for the organization. Obviously, as the goals are modified with the agreement of the board, the new list of goals is posted to BPM Part 2.

BPM Part 3 also contains information that may influence your meeting agenda. Notice that in Section 3.6 of our template, we include language about how the board will conduct its meetings, including setting the schedule of board meetings well in advance, how materials will be sent to the board members prior to the meetings, what the meetings will contain in the way of substance, and so on. Following the instructions in Section 3.6 is one of the first ways in which your board can honor the role of the BPM in guiding the way the board does business.

Use It to Guide Committee Work

Committees do the work of the board and give focus to the policies that are within their scope. As issues and questions arise, they are usually referred to a committee, where they can be researched and discussed before being presented to the full board. And, if a committee recommends a board policy to cover a particular issue or circumstance, it should bring the policy forward in language suitable for the appropriate section of the BPM. For example, if the finance committee determines that more guidance is needed in the area of, say, long-term financial commitments, it should identify which section of the BPM (Section 5.2 in the template) should contain the policy and then draft the language for presentation to the board.

Keep the BPM and the Board Perspective at the Policy Level

The Board Member's Playbook consists mainly of practice exercises for a board that has adopted the Policy Governance model and that has a policy manual. Each exercise in the *Playbook* begins with a scenario that describes a situation that the board is confronting. The process that Carver and Charney advise using to inform the thinking of the board includes a series of questions, such as whether the situation requires a board-level policy or whether it can be handled by the CEO within the existing policy structure. At the end of each exercise, after the reader has answered the questions, is the statement "You are now ready for the full board discussion and decision." It is a clear reminder that issues and potential policies should be vetted before precious board time is used to discuss and decide them.

Just as a golfer tries to establish a "muscle memory" that is repeatable in any situation, so too a board wants to adopt a reliable process for the way it reviews and decides on situations that arise. Whether or not you adopt a detailed approach like that laid out in the *Playbook*, you will want your approach to revolve around a policy manual like a BPM. Once the BPM has assumed that role in your governance framework, you will be safely into the third leg of the roadmap. Is the issue something that the board should be addressing, or is it better left to the CEO? If it is the board's concern, is there a policy in the BPM that already covers it? If not, what is the right policy, how should it be articulated, and where in the BPM should it go?

Once your governance "muscles" are accustomed to working with the BPM, you will gain confidence in the repeatability of the process and in the reliability of the BPM as the centerpiece in your governance model. Your agendas will be filled with issues that are worthy of the board's attention, your new members will be productive early in their tenures, and your board will survive changes in key people like your CEO or your chair.

Keep the BPM Manageable

Once you have developed your BPM and feel that it is integrated into your governance structure, it is time to leverage its role and its full range of benefits. Remember that the BPM is both comprehensive and concise. On the one hand, you want the BPM to cover the full range of the board's standing policies. In this sense, the "voice" of the board is more of a chorus than a solo. On the other hand, you want the size of the BPM to be manageable. Some policies require the preparation of related documents, which can be extensive in length. Embedding these documents in the BPM can expand its size beyond the twelve to twenty pages that we recommend. For example, some boards have long conflict of interest statements that must be signed annually by each board member. In such cases, we recommend storing the conflict of interest statements in a separate file and simply including in the BPM (1) the requirement that each board member sign the statement, (2) which version of the statement is current, and (3) the file where it will be stored.

Other documents that may be cited in the BPM and stored elsewhere include:

- Board profile (a description of desirable board member skills, diversity, and experience that guides the governance [nominating] committee in its selection of new board members)
- Annual affirmation statement
- Strategic plan
- CEO succession plan
- Specific processes that many be too wordy for the BPM, such as:
  - Nominations
  - Board-sponsored awards

The Board Reference Book

Most boards of large organizations will have several of these related documents that they will want to file separately and simply refer to in the BPM. For ease of access to these documents, we highly recommend that the board prepare a Board Reference Book (BRB), which will be available to the board members at each board meeting. In addition to the documents just listed, we recommend that the following documents be placed in the BRB:

- Articles of incorporation
- Bylaws

- Board member affirmation statements (annual commitment from each member)
- Minutes of last several meetings
- Organization budget
- Organization charts
- Board member résumés
- Contact information—board and staff
- Selected legal documents
- Other documents as appropriate

The BRB is normally maintained in a three-ring binder for ease of updating. We have worked with boards that have endeavored to supply a copy of the BRB to each member and then send updates to the BRB on a periodic basis. But, while some board members will dutifully post the latest updates, most board members would rather not be bothered. Especially for medium- to large-sized boards, this frequent updating can be a burden on the CEO and the staff as well as on the board members. Typically, the CEO's assistant can efficiently maintain two or three copies of the BRB and make them available as references during board meetings.

Most organizations have an Internet web site, which is an excellent way to afford access to key documents, both for the public and for board members. Some boards have emphasized disclosure of their operations and financial situations and have made copies of documents such as the bylaws, financial statements, and board minutes available on their web sites. Some states have open meeting laws and disclosure requirements that dictate what certain nonprofit boards must make available to the public. Your degree of disclosure will depend on your situation and the rules of the state in which you operate. However, where it is feasible, we recommend that you maintain a secure site for your board members, which they alone can access and where you can maintain a current copy of all the BRB documents.

We also have seen boards make their BPMs available to the public. This is an excellent way for the board to demonstrate its commitment to excellence and its transparency of operation. Normally, the BPM will not contain confidential matters, and, particularly for member organizations, disclosing the BPM will give both the members and the public confidence that the organization is in good hands.

✧

You are in one sense at the end of the journey that we lay out in the roadmap, but we hope that you appreciate that it is more accurate to say that this third and last leg of the journey really has no end. To borrow again from Mr. Churchill, you truly are at the end of a beginning, the beginning of operations under a new model of governance that reflects on a broad scale the best practices in nonprofit governance. We are confident that you can get there. We have seen many nonprofits follow the roadmap to good governance, and we describe four such organizations in Chapter 12.

CHAPTER 12

The Roadmap Taken: Four Case Histories

Two roads diverged in a wood, and I—I took the one less traveled by, And that has made all the difference.

—Robert Frost, "The Road Not Taken"

We have acknowledged that the majority of boards do not have a policy manual like a BPM. Nor is the number that have followed the roadmap particularly large. In a sense, therefore, with apologies to Mr. Frost, ours is a roadmap less traveled by. We would like that statistic to change, however, because we see that taking this roadmap can make all the difference.

Introducing Fellow Travelers

In the preceding chapters, we have presented our case for following the roadmap to good governance. In this chapter, we would like to tell you about four organizations that took this journey, the

161

same four organizations that were introduced in Chapter 1. They were chosen based on the diversity of their missions, their stage of development (age), and the approach that they took to the road-map. They are listed here along with their missions.

Miriam's Kitchen, Washington, DC: To provide individualized services that address the causes and consequences of homelessness in an atmosphere of dignity and respect, both directly and through facilitating connections in the Washington, DC, community.[1]

The Translational Genomics Research Institute (TGen), Phoenix, Arizona: To develop earlier diagnostics and smarter treatments through genomic research.[2]

The Association of Graduates (AOG), West Point, New York: To serve West Point and its graduates.[3]

World Vision Inc., Seattle, Washington: Dedicated to working with children, families, and their communities worldwide to enable them to reach their full potential by tackling the causes of poverty and injustice.[4]

These organizations have very different missions that affect the lives of very different constituencies. They are unlike in size, age, complexity, and geographical reach. The profiles of their boards are also different, as are their bylaws. Yet for all of their dissimilarities, these organizations share the common experience of following the roadmap that is laid out in this book. To be sure, the length of time and the resources expended along the way varied widely among these nonprofits—from a matter of weeks for Miriam's Kitchen to almost eighteen months for the AOG. Yet each of them has a functioning BPM that operates as the voice of its board.

We offer brief summaries of these organizations and their journey to developing a BPM as testimony to the flexibility and versatility of the roadmap. While we argue that the roadmap can fit almost any nonprofit, we don't prescribe the length of the journey or the duration of the steps that each organization will take along the way. As these stories will demonstrate, the time required to complete the three legs of the roadmap will vary with the organization. What stays constant are the benefits that accrue from having taken the route.

A Heart for Homeless People, a Head for Good Governance: Miriam's Kitchen

Since 1983, Miriam's Kitchen has served homeless people in the Foggy Bottom area of northwest Washington, DC. Starting by serving meals to a handful of guests, this faithful organization has become a source of hot food for hundreds of people on a daily basis. Its mission is to "provide individualized services that address the causes and consequences of homelessness in an atmosphere of dignity and respect, both directly and through facilitating connections in the Washington, DC, community."[5] In 2005, for example, Miriam's Kitchen served over 50,000 meals, a feat made possible by 13,000 hours of volunteer time from a cross section of people in the Washington, DC, metropolitan area. Every weekday, neither rain, nor snow, nor gloom of early morning (nor even holidays) has kept Miriam's from serving a hot breakfast to its guests.

Miriam's also employs three full-time case managers who help guests with a myriad of issues, including jobs, health care, food stamps, and housing. Arnold's Place, one of Miriam's programs, provides four men with a stable living environment while they work with case managers to find permanent solutions to their employment and housing problems. There's also an after-breakfast program that includes activities like painting, poetry, creative writing, literary discussion groups, sewing, and yoga.

Arriving After a Rough Ride

By most definitions, Miriam's Kitchen is a successful operation that is addressing a real need in the nation's capital, but its road to where it is today has been anything but smooth. Since its inception, Miriam's has been confronted with all manner of challenges. From 1994 to 1999, for example, there were six different kitchen directors and a revolving door for other key staff members. One kitchen director was attacked by a guest and hospitalized. Two kitchen directors lasted only a few months on the job.

Another challenge is trying to keep programs operating continually and smoothly while using volunteer labor. Miriam's has seen its ministry as more than simply feeding its guests, and it has endeavored over the years to implement programs that supplement the breakfast program and add food for the minds as well the stomachs. These supplementary programs require constant follow-through and are not easily run on a volunteer basis. Many of them have been started, only to stop weeks or months later because of the loss of a key person or a lack of traction within the community.

Nor has raising funds been an easy task over the years. While there is no shortage of people in the DC area who are willing to help homeless people, the need for a consistent flow of cash keeps the pressure on the board and the staff to husband their resources and communicate with their donors. That the revenues from various sources have grown steadily, especially in the last several years, is a credit to the organization's persistence and planning, a large part of which comes from board members.

Rewarding Faithfulness in Service; Looking for Excellence in Governance

Despite all the difficulties that Miriam's has endured over the years, it has become a healthy, vibrant organization. "As I read about Miriam's in its early years," remarks Scott Schenkelberg, the current executive director, "I'm sure that people wondered then if we would ever become an adult. It seems that for several stretches in time, this organization was fueled by nothing but true grit."

From the beginning, the source of much of the grit was the board of directors. The bylaws originally set the board at seven people, which was increased to sixteen in 2003. The directors at Miriam's are not your semiannual-come-to-meeting crowd. They are among the hundreds of volunteers who stand at the food lines, work with guests, and petition for funds. They also meet as a board as frequently as once a month.

In 2006, the board members sensed that they could do a better job of governing Miriam's, which had become an adult organization. "We have always had board members who were passionate for the mission of Miriam's Kitchen," indicated Melissa Williams, the board chair. "They are as committed a group as I've ever worked with. But we were nearing a quarter century of service, and we needed a model of governance that would keep up with our growth and leverage the talent and dedication of our board members."

Her response to this need was to devote the entire agenda for the annual board retreat to discussing ways to improve the governance of Miriam's. The retreat generated many ideas and identified several best practices that the board wanted to implement. However, the number and breadth of the proposed changes that came out of the retreat made it necessary to prioritize these changes for development and implementation. Fortunately, the retreat agenda included the description of the roadmap and how the BPM could provide an efficient way to (1) implement the changes in an orderly way and (2) adopt a flexible and durable framework on which to build Miriam's governance model.

"We saw the process of developing the BPM as a way for us to assess where we are now and to give us a clear view of where we needed new policies," said Ms. Williams.

The board agreed and committed to support a task force that had the job of drafting the initial BPM and presenting it to the board. The executive director took the lead in writing it, and, using our template (Appendix A), he prepared a draft for the task force in approximately ten hours. This rough draft was e-mailed to the task force, and less than two weeks later, the task force met to discuss the version of the BPM that would be sent to the board. During this meeting, the group concluded that most of the BPM— the portion that dealt with the basic principles of governance— was good to go to the board. The group also felt that the BPM could reflect some policies that seemed to be in force, but that had not been written down. Finally, the task force identified a half-dozen policies that it considered good candidates for the BPM, but that would require considerable board discussion before they could be adopted.

Two weeks after the meeting of the task force, the draft BPM was e-mailed to the board. At the next board meeting, because the board had already committed to the BPM (the first leg of the roadmap), the members carried out a constructive review, supporting most of what the task force had recommended, but deferring a decision on sections where they felt that more study was needed. At the end of the meeting, which took place six weeks after the board retreat, the board approved the BPM and moved into the third leg of the roadmap

"It was like we had installed one of those organizer systems in our board's governance closet," said Ms. Williams. "We still have a healthy to-do list for policies in the future, but our BPM serves not only to help prioritize the policies to develop, but also to communicate the existing policies to our CEO and his staff. We are becoming comfortable with it, and we intend to keep it as our primary point of reference for all we do as a board."

Leveraging the Medical, Educational, and Economic Promise of the Biosciences: TGen

On February 7, 2002, Arizona Governor Jane Hull assembled more than fifty visionary leaders at the Capitol to discuss the feasibility of making a statewide push into the new economy of the biosciences. The group's focus centered on establishing a one-of-a-kind research institute to serve as a catalyst for medical, educational, and economic gain.

The visionaries from science, medicine, government, and business who met that day indicated that not only was the idea feasible, but it also would provide a unique springboard for Arizona's entry into this thriving and rapidly expanding sector. The group set about rallying others behind its shared vision. And rally they did—to the tune of $120 million in commitments from various public and private organizations. Less than a year after the initial gathering in the governor's office, the Translational Genomics Research Institute (TGen) began operating, and Arizona's statewide push into the biosciences became a reality.

Brilliant Scientist, Proven Leader, but New to Governance

TGen's research platform rested on the relatively new field of translational research, which leverages the achievements of the Human Genome Project for early diagnoses and innovative treatments for many leading diseases and disorders. While the venture offered great promise, there were a number of significant challenges, such as recruiting talented researchers, building a responsive administrative infrastructure, and establishing an effective board of directors. To meet these challenges, the state of Arizona recruited native son Dr. Jeffrey Trent, an internationally known scientist, to serve as TGen's founding president and scientific director. Respected and well known, Dr. Trent had most recently built a world-class research program at the National Human Genome Research Institute, the government arm of the National Institutes of Health that successfully led the completion of the Human Genome Project. His agreement to lead TGen played no small role in gathering support for the venture.

Dr. Trent's reputation and scientific vision enabled him to recruit some of the best minds in the fields of genomics and medicine, and TGen was off to a quick start programmatically. But, while Dr. Trent was well equipped to handle the scientific and administrative sides of TGen, he had had only modest experience with the governance structure that had been established for the institute. The bylaws allowed for thirty board members, seven of whom were allocated to those organizations that had provided the initial funding for the venture. These included the state of Arizona, the city of Phoenix, the state's three major universities, the Salt River Pima tribe of Native Americans, and a major local foundation. The profile of the board of directors read like a Who's Who in the State of Arizona, including the governor, the mayor of Phoenix, three university presidents, and twenty other high-profile individuals.

"I had worked in many different research environments, but never with a nonprofit board of this caliber," said Dr. Trent. "The stature of the board members underscored the importance of TGen's success and the need to ensure that this powerful and multitalented team was working together."

TGen Follows the Roadmap

The newly formed TGen board elected José Cárdenas, a prominent attorney in Phoenix, as its chairman. In Mr. Cárdenas, Dr. Trent found an ally who fully understood the benefits of adopting a strong governance model and developing a BPM to ensure that TGen's board had a vehicle for implementing best practices for nonprofit organizations.

"We viewed our board as a tremendous asset," said Mr. Cárdenas. "The challenge lay in leveraging its strengths and talents while balancing the disparate personalities of its well-known members. We were convinced that the process of developing the BPM would give us a way to outline the expectations for the board and place everyone on the same page early."

Soon after the board's creation, Dr. Trent and Mr. Cárdenas assembled a team of staff members and consultants to begin work on the BPM. They also formed an advisory group selected from among TGen's board of directors to provide feedback on both the overall governance model and the specific policies being incorporated in the BPM.

The team started from scratch, as the board had only one meeting under its belt—a gathering that had been more ceremonial than substantive. The blank slate confronting it, however, provided the team with an opportunity to develop a congruent set of principles and policies without having to undo old ones. The creation of the advisory group to ensure director involvement proved invaluable. The advisors anticipated potential issues arising from the BPM structure, which allowed the team to modify its outline prior to presenting it to the full board.

At the second board meeting, less than two months after the team began its work, the board agreed on the concept of the BPM. Three months later, it approved the first version. A living document, the BPM has since undergone refinement as the board continually adapts to keep pace with TGen's steady growth and the dynamism of the bioscience field. And while the board roster has changed over time, the résumés of its newest members are no less impressive, and their support of TGen is no less passionate. There remains, therefore, the need to leverage their experience and talent and keep them working in unison.

"The BPM established a necessary framework, provided a singular focus from the beginning, and served us well through the critical first few years," said Mr. Cárdenas. "It will continue to be the centerpiece of TGen's governance structure as we go forward."

As the BPM has served the board, so too has TGen served its constituencies—by driving innovative research and discovery in the areas of science and health care, supporting local and statewide economic growth, and serving as a cornerstone for bioscience expansion throughout the state of Arizona. The words of Arizona's current governor, Janet Napolitano (herself an active member of the TGen board and an ardent supporter of its mission and vision), say it well:

> TGen and the possibilities it represents are among the most exciting developments Arizona has seen in years. Thanks to TGen researchers and their collaborators—across the state, nationally and around the world—Arizona is home to bioscience initiatives that hold the potential of improving lives all over the world.

Serving West Point and the Long Gray Line: The Association of Graduates of the United States Military Academy at West Point

For over two hundred years, the United States Military Academy at West Point has been producing officers for the U.S. Army. The prestigious parade of West Point graduates is known as the Long Gray Line, and it includes the likes of Lee, Grant, Pershing, MacArthur, Eisenhower, and Bradley. Though these great generals have all passed into the shadows, there are close to 50,000 members of the Long Gray Line who are still very much alive and who comprise an active and committed alumni.

During the Civil War, West Point graduates fought for both the North and the South, and almost all major battles had a West Pointer commanding at least one side and often both sides. Following the Civil War, a group gathered at West Point to form the Association of Graduates (AOG) with the purpose of bringing together those West Pointers, many of them classmates, who had waged war against one another. After the Civil War generation moved on, the AOG became a modest organization that served mainly to allow networking among graduates and help with class reunions. With the end of the Cold War in the early 1990s, however, the pressures on the federal budget in general and on the military budget in particular forced West Point to look for supplementary funds to maintain the margin of excellence that had characterized the academy for almost 200 years. It turned to the AOG to communicate its needs to the graduates and to encourage them to support their alma mater.

Two-Pronged Strategy to Recreate the AOG

Although the AOG was quick to respond to the call for help, its leaders realized that more was needed than simply canvassing the graduates for funds. As dedicated as the Long Gray Line was to West Point, for almost two centuries the academy had received its funding from the federal government. While other schools had well-organized development offices for contacting graduates for contributions, the AOG had only a modest staff with little orientation toward fund-raising. The AOG leadership knew that the AOG couldn't simply flip a switch and become a development organization. It needed to establish a firmer base among the graduates before they would be comfortable with pitches for money.

Tom Dyer was on the AOG Board of Trustees from the late 1980s and eventually became chairman in 2002. "We needed to become more professional in all aspects of serving our graduates as well as our school," Dyer described. "The academy had changed, the profile of the graduates had changed, and technology had changed. We needed to appreciate these dynamics and adjust our organization and our thinking at AOG to relate to the new generation."

It took a few years, but by the time West Point was ready to celebrate its bicentennial in 2002, it did so with the help of a well-organized, focused AOG. Since 1998, for example, the AOG has raised almost $300 million in general contributions and another $120 million for facilities for cadet activities, athletics, and academics, including a state-of-the-art center for combating terrorism, a Center for the Professional Military Ethic, and several academic chairs.

Playing Catch-Up with Governance

"Although we were pleased with the progress of AOG in serving the academy and the Long Gray Line, we were still operating with an antiquated governance structure, which was becoming a real drag on our efficiency," said Dyer. "Besides, if we were to expect excellence in our organization, we needed to establish and maintain it at the board level."

To address this problem, Dyer formed a task force to look into best practices in the governance of nonprofits and report back to the board what it should do to incorporate them. At the time the task force was formed, there were fifty-six members of the AOG board of trustees, the chairman was the CEO, and the board committees were essentially directing the AOG staff along the various functional lines. Because of the unwieldy number of board members, decisions were made by the executive committee, which comprised the AOG officers and the committee chairs.

Ted Stroup, Lt. Gen. USA retired, who was on the board in the late 1990s and who would later succeed Dyer as chairman, recalls, "We had a row of silos with our committees and far too much dependence on the chair as the CEO. And the executive committee was the de facto board. Our governance structure and processes needed a substantial overhaul."

Following the Roadmap

Dyer's task force agreed. It came back with a series of changes, most of which required changes in the bylaws. The board listened and acted. After a long season of selling the changes to the members of the Long Gray Line, the new bylaws were adopted in 2005 and implemented on January 1, 2006. One of those changes in the bylaws was a requirement that the board develop a BPM by the end of the first year. Knowing how the BPM development process can help establish and ingrain sound principles of governance, the task force insisted that the bylaws include this feature. Accordingly, soon after the new, streamlined board of sixteen members was sworn in on January 1, 2006, the new governance committee began the process of developing the BPM. It started with the template shown in Appendix A. The role of coordinator for developing the BPM fell to a senior staff person who was assigned to work with the committee. He began to flesh out the template with available data and with input received from the functional areas at AOG. After several reviews and revisions through e-mails and conference calls, the governance committee presented the draft BPM to the board, which approved the first version almost nine months after the governance committee began its initial work with the template.

As General Stroup describes, "I had several goals when I took over as chairman, one of which was to 'strive for excellence in our governance role.' The BPM development process allowed us to honor that commitment and attain that goal. It gave us a systematic basis for addressing best practices in nonprofit governance, and it is keeping those best practices in front of us as we carry out our fiduciary responsibilities."

West Pointers have immense pride in their school, and as the AOG has established more efficient ways to link with the Long Gray Line, it continues to motivate its members to give their time, talents, and money back to the academy. For its part, the AOG board has taken seriously its job of governing in the twenty-first century and has established high standards for its own performance that it intends to keep. Integrating the BPM into its governance model will help the AOG board meet those standards of excellence. Strong leadership is a characteristic that West Point expects of the members of the Long Gray Line in various venues and situations—and now even in the boardroom of its Association of Graduates.

Targeting Poverty and Injustice Throughout the World: World Vision

World Vision is a Christian humanitarian organization dedicated to working with children, families, and their communities worldwide to enable them to reach their full potential by tackling the causes of poverty and injustice. From its simple beginnings in 1953 as a one-man commitment to help Korean children orphaned in the Korean War, World Vision International has grown into one of the largest nonprofits in the world. During fiscal year 2006, World Vision/US, the largest partner among approximately 100 national organizations within World Vision International, had $944 million in revenues and a staff of 1,047.

A New President Gets It—As Does His Board

Richard Stearns became the fifth president of World Vision/US in the fall of 1998. He moved from the chief executive position at Lenox China and had never worked for a nonprofit board of directors. But Rich knew that a great nonprofit requires a great board. So he and his board chair, the Rev. Dr. John Huffman, agreed to have a board development workshop as part of Rich's first board meeting.

I (Bob) was asked to facilitate that daylong workshop on best practices in governance. Among the twenty or so topics discussed was a Board Policies Manual (BPM). The World Vision board was unanimous in supporting the BPM concept and requested that the BPM development be given a high priority.

Opting for the Fast Track

Dr. Huffman, exercising his role as manager of the board, said at the end of the World Vision board meeting, "Let's have the first draft ready for our next meeting." With such a complex organization and a rookie CEO, that was a tall order. But within days, Rich (the CEO) scheduled a day with John, a veteran World Vision executive, and me in order to draft an initial version of the BPM.

In preparation for the exercise, John had dutifully taken all the board minutes and resolutions for the last several years and neatly organized them into a full four-inch loose-leaf notebook. I remember thinking that he must have written rules for the military, as that notebook had an extremely elaborate numbering system. In John's mind, *it* was the board policies manual. But Rich and I (and soon, John) agreed that (1) no board member would read those hundreds of pages, (2) most of those old policies were written for a specific event or time period, and (3) the policies provided no current guidance to the board or the CEO. So we set a goal of twenty pages maximum for a new BPM and got to work using a template similar to the one in Appendix A of this book. The new BPM would eventually supersede all the verbiage in that thick notebook.

It's All About Results

The World Vision board did get its draft BPM at its next meeting. It was one way for the new CEO to demonstrate to his board that he (1) knew how to respond to a board request, (2) wanted to help the board to excel and to focus on governance policy, and (3) intended to use this BPM as a way to clarify the roles of the board and its CEO and to keep the organization on its proper strategic course.

Rich completed eight years as the World Vision CEO in 2006. Looking back at that daylong meeting on the BPM, he said, "Our attention to governance in general and the BPM in particular revolutionized our board—and I feel that I am the greatest beneficiary. I am still on a honeymoon with the board after eight years!"

But improving the governance at World Vision is not the only contribution Rich has made in his eight years as CEO. In fiscal year 2006, this amazing organization distributed $820 million in goods and services to the poor around the world, an increase of $545 million (nearly triple) over the year when Rich was selected as CEO.

Jim Beré was on the board in 1998 when the decision was made to develop the BPM and at this writing is the board chair. He says of the BPM, "This document gives a structure and focus for everything we do as a board. We have wonderful people on the board who are passionate for our vision. I feel personally responsible for helping them apply their multiple talents to the governance process with a minimum of wasted energy. The BPM allows me to do just that. It frees me up to manage effectively and evenly across the board. It is a board chair's best friend."

✧

These case studies are not isolated examples of organizations that stumbled into developing a BPM. Each organization was aware of the effort and commitment that was required to follow the roadmap. So, too, was each aware of the contribution that the BPM would bring to its governance function. As different as they are in size and scope of service, these organizations share a common framework for bringing excellence to their governance function. Each of these organizations is well served by a board whose voice is clearly and consistently heard through its BPM.

18 Months Later—Does it Work?

So you've done it. Your board has approved the initial BPM, and you have updated it at each meeting since then—five times now. The committees are bringing their recommendations to the board meetings in the form of policy language, and your CEO is finding the BPM helpful in clarifying her job. She and your board used the BPM process to conduct her annual evaluation, and your latest selection of new board members took advantage of your BPM board profile. Although there are still some policies that you have not implemented, like, for example, the Annual Affirmation Statement (some directors continue to want to make changes in it), you think the whole BPM thing is here to stay.

We asked in Chapter 11, "Are we there yet?" Well, we have yet to find a board that "is there" in terms of board perfection, but we do believe that you can get miles down the road within twelve to eighteen months. If you are there, you have learned that it takes the support of the board chair and the CEO, working in advance of each meeting and reminding the board of its policies in the BPM, to experience steady progress. And it may have taken another board member, perhaps you, to prod and encourage along the way.

After all this, are you a better board? Or have you simply gone through an exercise to prove your ability to write policies and organize them in a manual? Are you really any better off with the BPM-centric governance model?

To answer that question, let's go back and look at the ways in which the experts suggest that you measure the quality of governance. Recall our discussion of how with nonprofits, there is no magic metric like Collins's sustained market performance and matched-pair analysis in *Good to Great*. And even if Good-to-Great actions apply to nonprofits, they pertain to the performance of the organization, not necessarily to its governance. Drilling down to measure the performance of a nonprofit board is another matter. As we pointed out in Chapter 1, however, there are ways to gauge the performance of nonprofit boards, albeit on a qualitative scale, by comparing their actions with a list of what experts considered to be best practices.

In Chapter 1 we offered three examples of such lists of best practices: the BoardSource Principles,[1] the Governance Matters Indicators,[2] and our own Attributes of Excellence. You may at this point choose to go back to those lists and compare how well you performed against them BBPM (before BPM) and ABPM (after BPM). You may want to hire a consultant or use some of the dozens of self-assessment instruments that can be downloaded from Internet sites. Or you may be satisfied with a general assessment from your board members.

However you choose to evaluate your performance as a board, we believe that your having followed the roadmap will give you a keener eye for the assessment. Your board members will also be more capable in their critiques. Further, and perhaps more important, you may very well enjoy the process of scoring yourselves. Good students tend to be excited about report card day, rather than begrudge it. As you honor your commitment to improve as a board, you will find that you and your colleagues are more adept at finding areas of improvement, but also more confident of your ability to deal with them.

If you are ready to take on more board development, we have included in Appendix B a list of several other "board tools" that we use as we engage with other boards. You can download these documents from the AMA website and tailor them to your organization's needs.

Is it worth it, this BPM that we have called the best "governance management system" available? The most honest response we can give is that organizations that have implemented the BPM as we have outlined it in this book would not think of going back to their old ways. The challenge is that your chairperson, CEO, and others who provided leadership will leave some day. Old habits will sneak back into your processes and meetings. It will take one or two champions of excellence to keep this "living document" at the fore-front and to mentor others on the use of the roadmap. We hope that you will be one of those champions. You can do it, and we hope we've helped.

Board Policies Manual (BPM) for ABC, Inc.*

Note: This version of the BPM was approved by the board on January 21, 2007, and reflects several changes from the previous version, which should be discarded.

Part 1: Introduction and Administration

This Board Policies Manual (BPM) contains all of the current standing (ongoing) policies adopted by the board of [ORGANIZATION] since the initial approval of the BPM on [INITIAL APPROVAL DATE].

1.1 Reasons for Adoption. The reasons for adopting this BPM include:

- Efficiency of having all ongoing board policies in one place
- Ability to quickly orient new board members to current policies

*An MS Word version of this template is available on the AMA website.

- Elimination of redundant or conflicting policies over time
- Ease of reviewing current policy when considering new issues
- Providing clear, proactive policies to guide the chief executive officer (CEO) and staff
- Modeling an approach to governance that other organizations might use

1.2 Consistency. Each policy in this document is expected to be consistent with the law, the articles of incorporation, and the by-laws, all of which have precedence over these board policies. Except for time-limited or procedural-only board decisions (approving minutes, electing an officer, etc.), which are recorded in regular board minutes, all standing policies shall be included or referred to in this document. The CEO is responsible for developing organizational and administrative policies and procedures that are consistent with this BPM.

1.3 Transition. Whether adopted part by part or as a complete document, as soon as some version of the BPM is voted on as the "one voice" of the board, those policies are deemed to supersede any past policy that might be found in old minutes unless a prior board resolution or contract obligates the organization with regard to a specific matter. If any actual or apparent conflict arises between the BPM and other policies or board resolutions, the matter shall be resolved by the chair or by the entire board as may be appropriate.

1.4 Changes. These policies are meant to be reviewed constantly and are frequently reviewed and refined. The CEO helps the board formulate new language in the BPM by distributing proposed changes in advance. When language is recommended for deletion, it is shown in ~~strike-through~~ format. Proposed new language is underlined. Each section with a proposed change can be preceded by the # sign to help readers quickly locate proposed changes. Any change to this BPM must be approved by the full board. Proposed changes may be submitted by any board member as well as by the CEO. In most cases, proposed changes shall be referred to and reviewed by the appropriate committee before being presented to the board for action. Whenever changes are adopted, a new document should be printed, dated, and quickly made available to the board and staff. The previous version should be kept on a disk for future reference if needed.

1.5 Specificity. Each new policy will be drafted to fit in the appropriate place within the BPM. Conceptually, policies should be drafted from the "outside in," i.e., the broadest policy statement should be presented first, then the next broadest, etc., down to the level of detail that the board finds appropriate for board action and below which management is afforded discretion as to how it implements the policies in this BPM.

1.6 Oversight Responsibility. Below are the parts, the committees primarily responsible for drafting and reviewing those parts, and the individuals given authority to interpret and make decisions within the scope of those policies:

Part/Section	Oversight Committee	Implementation Authority
1. Introduction	Governance Committee	CEO
2. Organization Essentials	Full Board	CEO
3. Board Structure and Processes	Governance Committee	Board Chair
4. Board–CEO/Staff Relationship	Executive Committee	Chair/CEO
5. Executive Parameters		
5.1 General Guidance	Governance Committee	CEO
5.2 Finance	Finance Committee	CEO
5.3 Programs	Program Committee	CEO
5.4 Advancement	Advancement Committee	CEO
5.5 Audit and Compliance	Audit and Compliance Committee	CEO
5.6 Miscellaneous	As appropriate	CEO

1.7 Maintenance of Policies. The secretary shall ensure that staff members record and publish all standing policies correctly. The

CEO or the CEO's designee shall maintain the policies file and provide updated copies to the board whenever the policies change, or upon request. The board will ask that legal counsel review this BPM biennially to ensure compliance with the law. Discrete documents referred to in the BPM will be kept in a three-ring notebook called the Board Reference Book.

Part 2: Organization Essentials

2.1 Our **vision** is . . .

2.2 Our **mission** is . . .

2.3 The **values** that guide everything we do are . . .

2.4 The **moral owners** to whom the board feels accountable (e.g., members, alumni, donors, or taxpayers) are . . .

2.5 The primary **beneficiaries** of our services are . . .

2.6 The major general **functions** and the approximate percentage of total effort that is expected to be devoted to each are . . .

2.7 The primary **strategies** by which we will fulfill our mission include . . .

2.8 The major organizational **goals** and monitoring indicators for the next three years are . . .

2.9 Strategic Plans. The board is expected to think strategically at all times. The CEO is expected to develop a staff strategic plan based on the policies in this BPM, update it as necessary, link major activities in the plan to the relevant sections of this BPM, and provide copies of the plan to the board for information by April 1 each year.

Part 3: Board Structure and Processes

3.1 Governing Style. The board will approach its task with a style that emphasizes outward vision rather than an internal preoccupation, encouragement of diversity in viewpoints, strategic leadership more than administrative detail, clear distinction of board and staff roles, and proactivity rather than reactivity. In this spirit, the board will:

    3.1.1 Enforce upon itself and its members whatever discipline is needed to govern with excellence. Discipline shall apply to matters such as attendance, respect for clarified roles, speaking to management and the public with one voice, and self-policing of any tendency to stray from the governance structure and processes adopted in these board policies.

    3.1.2 Be accountable to its stakeholders and the general public for competent, conscientious, and effective accomplishment of its obligations as a body. It will allow no officer, individual, or committee of the board to usurp this role or hinder this commitment.

    3.1.3 Monitor and regularly discuss the board's own processes and performance, seeking to ensure the continuity of its governance functions by selection of capable directors, orientation and training, and evaluation.

    3.1.4 Be an initiator of policy, not merely a reactor to staff initiatives. The board, not the staff, will be responsible for board performance.

3.2 Board Job Description. The job of the board is to lead the organization toward the desired performance and ensure that that performance occurs. The board's specific contributions are unique to its trusteeship role and necessary for proper governance and management. To perform its job, the board shall:

    3.2.1 Determine the mission, values, strategies, and major goals/outcomes, and hold the CEO accountable for developing a staff strategic plan based on these policies.

    3.2.2 Determine the parameters within which the CEO is expected to achieve the goals/outcomes.

3.2.3 Monitor the performance of the organization relative to the achievement of the goals/outcomes within the executive parameters.

3.2.4 Maintain and constantly improve all ongoing policies of the board in this BPM.

3.2.5 Select, fairly compensate, nurture, evaluate annually, and, if necessary, terminate a CEO, who functions as the board's sole agent.

3.2.6 Ensure financial solvency and integrity through policies and behavior.

3.2.7 Require periodic financial and other external audits to ensure compliance with the law and with good practices.

3.2.8 Evaluate and constantly improve our board's performance as the governing board, and set expectations for board members' involvement as volunteers.

3.3 Board Member Criteria. In nominating members for the board, the board Governance Committee shall be guided by the board profile that is kept current in the Board Reference Book.

3.4 Orientation. Prior to election, each nominee shall be given this BPM along with adequate briefings on the role of the board, officers, and staff and an overview of programs, plans, and finances. Soon after election, each new board member will be given more comprehensive orientation material and training.

3.5 Chair's Role. The job of the chair is, primarily, to maintain the integrity of the board's processes. The chair "manages the board." The chair is the only board member authorized to speak for the board, other than in rare and specifically board-authorized instances.

The chair ensures that the board behaves in a manner consistent with its own rules and those legitimately imposed upon it from outside the organization. Meeting discussion content will be those issues that, according to board policy, clearly belong to the board to decide, not to staff.

The authority of the chair consists only in making decisions on behalf of the board that fall within and are consistent with any reasonable interpretation of board policies in Parts 3 and 4 of this BPM. The chair has no authority to make decisions beyond policies created by the board. Therefore, the chair has no authority to supervise or direct the CEO's work, but is expected to maintain close communication with, offer advice to, and provide encouragement to the CEO and staff on behalf of the board.

3.6 Board Meetings. Board events often will include time for guest presenters, interaction with staff and beneficiaries, board training, and social activities, as well as business sessions. Policies that are intended to improve the process for planning and running meetings follow:

3.6.1. The schedule for board meetings shall be set two years in advance.

3.6.2. The CEO shall work with the chair and the committee chairs in developing agendas, which, along with background materials for the board and committees, monitoring reports, the CEO's recommendations for changes in the BPM, previous minutes, and other such materials, shall be mailed to all board members approximately two weeks in advance of board meetings.

3.6.3 Minutes and the updated BPM shall be sent to board members within 14 days of board meetings.

3.6.4 Regular board meetings shall be held ___ times a year in the months of _____, _____, and _____, preceded by a reminder notice approximately 30 days in advance of the meeting date. The _____ meeting shall include a review of the planning and budgeting for the upcoming year. The _____ meeting shall include a review of the performance of the CEO and the organization for the past year. Special meetings of the board can be called according to the bylaws [if this process is not in the bylaws, define it here].

3.6.5 The Governance Committee shall prepare a meeting evaluation form for completion by each board member who attends the board meeting. The completed forms shall be reviewed, analyzed, and summarized by the Governance Committee, which shall report the results of the meeting evaluation to the board members within two weeks of the board meeting.

3.7 Standing Committees. Committees help the board be effective and efficient. They speak "to the board" and not "for the board." Unless authorized by the whole board, a committee may not exercise authority that is reserved to the whole board by the bylaws or by the laws of [*name of state*] governing not-for-profit organizations. Committees are not created to advise or exercise authority over staff. Once committees are created by the board, the board chair shall recommend committee chairs and members for one-year terms, subject to board approval. The board chair and the CEO are *ex officio* members of all committees except the Audit and Compliance Committee. The CEO shall assign one senior staff member to assist with the work of each committee.

    3.7.1 *Governance Committee.* This committee shall recommend policies to the board pertaining to governance issues and processes, including the orientation and training of new board members, the evaluation and improvement of the contribution of individual board members and officers, and the recommendation of bylaw changes. The committee will also develop a roster of potential board members based on the board profile, and will nominate all board members and officers.

    3.7.2 *Finance Committee.* This committee shall develop and recommend to the board those financial principles, plans, and courses of action that provide for mission accomplishment and organizational financial well-being. Consistent with this responsibility, it shall review the annual budget and submit it to the board for its approval. In addition, the committee shall make recommendations with regard to the level and terms of indebtedness, cash management, investment policy, risk management, financial monitoring and reports, employee benefit plans, signatory authority for expenditures, and other policies for inclusion in the BPM that the committee determines are advisable for effective financial management.

3.7.3 *Audit and Compliance Committee.* This committee shall oversee the organization's internal accounting controls; recommend external auditors for board approval; review the external auditors' annual audit plan; and review the annual report, the management letter, and the results of the external audit. The committee, or its delegate, shall have an annual private conversation with the auditor. In addition, the committee shall be responsible for oversight of regulatory compliance, policies and practices regarding corporate responsibility, and ethics and business conduct–related activities, including compliance with all federal, state, and local laws governing tax-exempt entities. The committee shall also oversee written conflict of interest policies and procedures for directors and officers (see tab __ of the Board Reference Book).

3.7.4 *Advancement Committee.* This committee shall study and recommend policies relating to communications and public relations as well as policies relating to raising financial and other resources for the organization.

3.7.5 *Programs Committee.* This committee shall study and recommend policies relating to all programs and services of the organization.

3.7.6 *Executive Committee.* This committee shall comprise the chair, other officers, and the chairs of the other committees in Section 3.7. Except for the actions enumerated below, it shall have the authority to act for the board on all matters so long as the Executive Committee determines that it would be imprudent to wait for the next board meeting to take such action. With respect to any action taken on behalf of the board, (1) the Executive Committee is required to report the action to the board within 10 days, and (2) the board must approve the action at the next board meeting.

The Executive Committee is not authorized to make decisions or to take action with respect to the following matters:

3.7.6.1 Dissolving the corporation

3.7.6.2 Hiring or firing the chief executive

3.7.6.3 Entering into major contracts or suing another entity

3.7.6.4 Making significant changes to a board-approved budget

3.7.6.5 Adopting or eliminating major programs

3.7.6.6 Buying or selling property

3.7.6.7 Amending the bylaws

3.7.6.8 Changing any policies that the board determines may be changed only by the board

3.7.7 Other committees as determined.

3.8 Advisory Groups, Councils, and Task Forces. To increase its knowledge base and depth of available expertise, the board supports the use of groups, councils, and task forces of qualified advisers. The term "task force" refers to any group appointed by the CEO or the chair to assist him or her in carrying out various time-limited goals and responsibilities. Although either the chair or the CEO may form a task force, he or she shall notify the board of its formation, purpose, and membership within 10 days of its formation. The CEO may assign a senior staff member to serve advisory groups. The board has established the following advisory groups:

3.8.1 (Name, membership, function, etc., of any advisory group the board creates.)

3.9 Board Members' Code of Conduct. The board expects of itself and its members ethical and businesslike conduct. Board members must offer unconflicted loyalty to the interests of the entire organization, superseding any conflicting loyalty such as that to family members, advocacy or interest groups, and other boards or staffs of which they are members. Board members must avoid any conflict of interest with respect to their fiduciary responsibility. There must be no self-dealing or conduct of private business or personal services between any board member and the organization except as procedurally controlled to assure openness, competitive opportunity, and equal access to "inside" information.

The board will make no judgments of the CEO or staff performance except as the performance of the CEO is assessed against explicit board policies and agreed-upon performance objectives.

Each board member is expected to complete and sign an Annual Affirmation Statement, which covers, *inter alia*, board conflicts of interest, in accordance with the laws of the state governing not-for-profit organizations, and other expectations of board members.

3.10 Board Finances. Every board member is expected to be a donor of record in each calendar year. Expenses incurred to fulfill board activities normally can be an individual tax deduction; however, any board member may submit for reimbursement any expenses incurred to attend board or committee meetings.

Part 4: Board–CEO/Staff Relationship

4.1 Delegation to the Chief Executive Officer (CEO). While the board's job is generally confined to establishing high-level policies, implementation and subsidiary policy development are delegated to the CEO.

    4.1.1 All board authority delegated to staff is delegated through the CEO, so that all authority and accountability of staff—as far as the board is concerned—is considered to be the authority and accountability of the CEO.

    4.1.2 Organization
Essentials policies (Part 2) direct the CEO to achieve certain results. Executive Parameters policies (Part 5) define the acceptable boundaries of prudence and ethics within which the CEO is expected to operate. The CEO is authorized to establish all further policies, make all

decisions, take all actions, and develop all activities as
long as they are consistent with any reasonable interpretation of the board's policies in this BPM.

4.1.3. The board may change its policies during any meeting,
thereby shifting the boundary between board and CEO
domains. Consequently, the board may change the latitude of choice given to the CEO, but so long as any
particular delegation is in place, the board and its members will respect and support the CEO's choices. This
does not prevent the board from obtaining information
in the delegated areas.

4.1.4 Except when a person or committee has been authorized
by the board to incur some amount of staff cost for
study of an issue, no board member, officer, or committee has authority over the CEO. Only officers or committee chairs may request information, but if such a
request—in the CEO's judgment—requires a material
amount of staff time or funds or is disruptive, it may be
refused.

4.2 CEO Job Description. As the board's single official link to
the operating organization, CEO performance will be considered
to be synonymous with organizational performance as a whole.
Consequently, the CEO's job contributions can be stated as performance in two areas: (a) organizational accomplishment of the
major organizational goals in Section 2.8, and (b) organization
operations within the boundaries of prudence and ethics established in board policies on Executive Parameters.

4.3 Communication and Counsel to the Board. With respect to
providing information and counsel to the board, the CEO shall
keep the board informed about matters essential to carrying out
its policy duties. Accordingly, the CEO shall:

4.3.1 Inform the board of relevant trends, anticipated adverse
media coverage, and material external and internal
changes, particularly changes in the assumptions upon
which any board policy has previously been established,

always presenting information in as clear and concise a format as possible.

4.3.2 Relate to the board as a whole except when fulfilling reasonable individual requests for information or responding to officers or committees duly charged by the board.

4.3.3 Report immediately any actual or anticipated material noncompliance with a policy of the board, along with suggested changes.

4.4 Monitoring Executive Performance. The purpose of monitoring is to determine the degree to which the mission is being accomplished and board policies are being fulfilled. Information that does not do this shall not be considered monitoring. Monitoring will be as automatic as possible, using a minimum of board time, so that meetings can be used to affect the future rather than to review the past. A given policy may be monitored in one or more of three ways:

4.4.1 *Direct board inspection:* Discovery of compliance information by a board member, a committee, or the board as a whole. This includes board inspection of documents, activities, or circumstances that allows a "prudent person" test of policy compliance.

4.4.2 *External report:* Discovery of compliance information by a disinterested, external person or firm who is selected by and reports directly to the board. Such reports must assess executive performance only against legal requirements or policies of the board, with suggestions from the external party as to how the organization can improve itself.

4.4.3 *CEO reports:* The CEO shall help the board determine what tracking data are available to measure progress in achieving the mission and goals and conforming with board policies. Currently the board requests these regular monitoring reports, in addition to any specific reports requested in other sections of the BPM:

4.4.3.1 Monthly: Informal CEO reports on achievements, problems, and board notices.

4.4.3.2 Quarterly: (a) A one- or two-page "dashboard" report showing agreed-upon key indicators that track designated financial and program results over a three-year period in graphic form; (b) other summary reports as the board may define in this BPM.

4.4.3.3 Semiannually: (a) Expense and revenue against budget report with comparison to previous year; (b) balance sheet; (c) cash flow projections; (d) membership statistics.

4.4.3.4 Annually: Within 45 days of the end of the fiscal year, (a) end-of-year expense and revenue against budget; (b) balance sheet; (c) staff organization chart (or whenever major changes are made); (d) other reports that the board may define in this BPM.

4.5 Annual Performance Review. A performance evaluation task force, comprising the board chair, the vice chair, and the chair of the Governance Committee, shall formally evaluate the CEO annually, based on achievement of organizational goals and any other specific goals that the board and the CEO have agreed upon in advance, as well as the CEO's own written self-evaluation and invited comments from all board members after they have seen the self-evaluation. The chair shall serve as chair of the task force. After meeting with the CEO, the task force will report on its review to the board, including recommendations on the CEO's compensation, which the Executive Committee or the board will then act upon.

During this process, the CEO and the board will agree on any specific, personal performance goals for the year ahead. These goals shall be documented in a letter to the CEO from the board chair and will be a primary basis for determining the CEO's performance at the end of the next year. At least every three years, the task force shall invite other input in a carefully planned "360" review, inviting feedback from staff, peers in our sector, and individuals outside the organization who have interacted with the CEO.

4.6 *Staff Compensation.* The CEO is expected to hire, train, motivate, compensate, and terminate staff in a professional and caring fashion. Salaries will be set at between X% and Y% of the mean for salaries in organizations of similar size, budget, and location. Benefits will include. . . . The CEO shall (a) develop and maintain an employee manual that is reviewed annually by competent legal counsel and (b) provide copies of this manual to the board for information around April 1 of each year.

4.7 *Staff Treatment.* With respect to treatment of paid and volunteer staff, the CEO may not cause or allow conditions that are inhumane, unfair, or undignified. Accordingly, he may not:

4.7.1 Discriminate among employees on other than clearly job-related, individual performance or qualifications.

4.7.2 Fail to take reasonable steps to protect staff from unsafe or unhealthy conditions.

4.7.3 Withhold from staff a due-process, unbiased grievance procedure.

4.7.4 Discriminate against any staff member for expressing an ethical dissent.

4.7.5 Prevent staff from grieving to the board when (a) internal grievance procedures have been exhausted and (b) the employee alleges that board policy has been violated to his or her detriment.

4.7.6 Fail to acquaint staff members with their rights under this policy.

4.8 *CEO Transitions.* At any time, the chair may appoint a transition task force to explore options and propose strategies and board policies related to succession and transition of the CEO and to facilitate any special needs of the outgoing and incoming CEOs and their families. The incumbent CEO shall give the board, if possible, a(n) ____-month notice of intent to leave that office. Any need for an acting or interim CEO will be determined by the board chair subject to board approval. The board chair is authorized, as soon as a vacancy or scheduled departure of the CEO is known, to appoint a search committee and committee chair. The search committee may include up to two people not on the board. The committee shall within 30 days recommend for board approval a position announcement, a recommendation on any search consultant, the appointment of a search secretary, and a budget for the search. The search committee shall present one or two qualified candidates to the full board for selection. A special task force appointed by the chair shall, at the time of selection, negotiate the new CEO's compensation and service agreement and give both the incumbent and the successor CEO any special performance priorities from the board. After he/she leaves the organization, the outgoing CEO may be given a paid role, but only with the approval of the new CEO in consultation with the officers and the board.

4.9 Board Reference Book and Web Site. In addition to reports that the CEO may choose to make to the board, the CEO shall develop and maintain a Board Reference Book with all pertinent documents to which board members might want to refer during board and committee meetings (e.g., articles, bylaws, organization chart, recent minutes, committee roster, list of key volunteers/consultants, board documents referred to in this BPM, etc.). In addition, the board requests that the CEO maintain, as funding is available, a secure Internet web site for board members to allow them to access relevant data and reports on a timely basis. The CEO shall notify board members as new key information is posted to the board web site.

Part 5: Executive Parameters

5.1 General Guidance. The purpose of the remainder of the BPM is to detail those executive parameters that will guide the CEO and the staff as they accomplish the mission. These parameters are intended to free the CEO and the staff to make timely decisions without undue board directives. The board expects that the CEO will do nothing that is illegal, unethical, or imprudent. Beyond these general parameters, the board details its executive parameters in the major sections that follow in Part 5.

5.2 Finance Parameters. The CEO must ensure that the financial integrity of the organization is maintained at all times; that proper care is exercised in the receiving, processing, and disbursing of funds; and that financial and nonfinancial assets are appropriately protected.

> 5.2.1 *Budgeting.* The budget during any fiscal period shall not (a) deviate materially from the board's goals and priorities listed in Part 2, (b) risk fiscal jeopardy, or (c) fail to show a generally acceptable level of foresight. Accordingly, the CEO may not cause or allow budgeting that:
>
> > 5.2.1.1 Contains too little detail to (a) enable accurate projection of revenues and expenses, (b) separate capital items from operational items, (c) monitor cash flow and subsequent audit trails, and (d) disclose planning assumptions.
> >
> > 5.2.1.2 Anticipates the expenditure in any fiscal year of more funds than are conservatively projected to be received in that period.
> >
> > 5.2.1.3 Reduces the current assets at any time to less than twice current liabilities or allows cash to drop below a safety reserve of $_____ at any time.
> >
> > 5.2.1.4 Provides less than $_____ for board prerogatives during the year, such as costs of the annual audit and board development.
> >
> > 5.2.1.5 Is not derived from the strategic plan.
>
> 5.2.2 *Financial Controls.* The CEO must exercise care in accounting for and protecting the financial assets of the organization. To this end, the CEO is expected to incorporate generally accepted accounting principles and internal controls in the financial systems that are employed in the organization. In addition, the CEO may not:

5.2.2.1 Receive, process, or disburse funds under controls insufficient to meet the board-appointed auditor's standards.

5.2.2.2 Approve an unbudgeted expenditure or commitment of greater than $_____ without the approval of the full board.

5.2.2.3 Approve an unbudgeted expenditure or commitment of greater than $_____ without the approval of the Finance Committee.

5.2.3 *Asset Protection.* The CEO may not allow assets to be unprotected, inadequately maintained, or unnecessarily risked. Accordingly, the CEO may not:

5.2.3.1 Fail to insure against theft and casualty losses to at least 80 percent of replacement cost and against liability losses to board members, staff, or the organization itself beyond the minimally acceptable prudent level.

5.2.3.2 Allow nonbonded personnel access to material amounts of funds.

5.2.3.3 Subject office equipment to improper wear and tear or insufficient maintenance.

5.2.3.4 Unnecessarily expose the organization, its board, or its staff to claims of liability.

5.2.3.5 Make any major purchase of over $_____ without sealed bids or some other demonstrably prudent method of acquisition of quality goods, or any purchase of over $_____ without a written record of competitive prices, or any purchase wherein normally prudent protection against conflict of interest has not been provided.

5.2.3.6 Acquire, encumber, or dispose of real property without board approval.

5.2.4 *Investment Principles.* The CEO may not invest or hold operating capital in insecure instruments, including uninsured checking accounts and bonds of less than AA rating, or in non-interest-bearing accounts, except where necessary to facilitate operational transactions.

5.3 Program Parameters. In general, the CEO is expected to establish, maintain, and eliminate programs and services to achieve the organization's mission and goals in the most effective and efficient manner.

    5.3.1 New programs should be projected to serve at least _____ people.

    5.3.2 New programs with an expected budget exceeding $_____ must be approved by the board. Those programs now approved include:

    5.3.3 Programs with costs of more than $_____ shall be assessed for effectiveness by an outside evaluator at least every three years, with a written report being made available to the board.

    5.3.4 Any program executed in partnership with another organization shall _____.

5.4 Advancement Parameters. The various efforts to represent the organization to the public (media, public relations, fundraising, new member recruitment, etc.) shall be integrated sufficiently so that the organization's brand/positioning in the external world is positive and effective.

    5.4.1 *Fund-Raising Strategy.* The CEO shall develop and maintain a fund-raising plan that, at a minimum, includes direct mail, major donor initiatives, planned giving, and Web-based giving. Such plan shall be provided to board members for review each March, along with results for each initiative. Total direct and indirect expenses for fund-raising shall not exceed 22 percent of the total budget.

        5.4.1.1 *Donor Bill of Rights.* The CEO shall develop a Donor Bill of Rights and provide the latest version to the board; this shall include, *inter alia*, the following restrictions: the CEO may not allow the names of donors to be revealed outside the organization, represent to a donor that an action will be taken that violates board policies, fail to honor a request from a donor as to how her/his contribution is to be allocated, fail to confirm receipt of a donor's contribution, or fail to send a donor an annual summary of donations.

    5.4.1.2 *Training.* The CEO shall ensure that appropriate members of the board and staff receive annual training in new fund-raising techniques and shall budget for such expenses.

5.4.2 *Public Affairs.* The CEO shall exercise care in representing that we are a charitable, mission-centered, listening organization and shall develop policies and procedures for communicating with primary stakeholders and the public at large in a way that reinforces that image.

    5.4.2.1 *Communications Plan.* The CEO shall develop and maintain a communications plan, shared with the board as appropriate, that describes how the organization will communicate with its various stakeholders. The plan shall identify the stakeholder segments, how the organization will both speak and listen to each segment, and who is allowed to speak for the organization. The plan shall also include the role of board members both as "listeners" and as "speakers" for the organization.

    5.4.2.2 *Communications Restrictions.* To preserve our image in the community, the CEO and any designee are the only spokespersons authorized to speak for the organization, and the chair is the only spokesperson for the board. None of the spokespersons may represent the organization in any way that is inconsistent with the policies in Part 2 of this BPM; make statements that may be perceived as supporting a political party or platform; be the author of an article, book, or publication that includes classified or sensitive information about the organization; or engage in lobbying activities at any governmental level without prior permission from the board.

5.5 Audit and Compliance Parameters. The CEO shall take the necessary steps to ensure the integrity of our systems and procedures; to see that they comply with all pertinent legal, regulatory, and professional requirements; and to report to the board any material variations or violations.

  5.5.1 *Annual External Audit.* An independent auditor will be hired and supervised by the Audit and Compliance Committee, after a careful selection and annual evaluation. The CEO shall work with the auditor to gain a clean opinion on the annual financial statements and respond in detail to items in the auditor's management letter concerning opportunities to improve systems and procedures related to financial controls.

  5.5.2 *Internal Compliance.* The CEO shall meet all requirements for complying with federal, state, or local laws and regulations. The CEO shall maintain a list of compliance actions and reports that are required of a nonprofit organization and periodically submit the list for inspection by the Audit and Compliance Committee. On a biennial basis, starting in FY____, the CEO shall contract for a legal review of the organization's compliance with the pertinent laws and regulations and make the results of the review available to the Audit and Compliance Committee, which, in turn, will report to the board on the overall status of the organization with respect to compliance matters, including any current problems or anticipated problems with regulatory authorities.

5.6 Miscellaneous.   [Include other policies that don't naturally fit into one of the other major sections.]

Supplemental Material Available on AMA Website

This appendix lists the supplemental materials (e.g., handouts, checklists, presentations, templates) that can be downloaded from the AMA website: www.amacombooks.org/go/goodgovnonprofits. We have used these materials to assist nonprofit leaders in developing effective policies and implementing best practices in nonprofit governance. Although these are basic versions of the documents, including the BPM template (Item 1), we are constantly refining them for particular organizations and situations. In a similar way, you are encouraged to tailor them to your organization and circumstances. Except for Item 2 (Board Presentation), which is a PowerPoint presentation, all documents are in MS Word.

	Document Title	Document Description
1	BPM Template	Version of BPM Template in Appendix A
2	Board Presentation	PowerPoint version of presentation to board recommending development of BPM
3	Principles for Nonprofit Self-Regulation	Summary of report of Panel on Nonprofit Sector with references to BPM template
4	Board Reference Book (BRB)	Purpose and recommended content of BRB
5	Strategic Planning Model for Nonprofits	Summary of roles and steps in a recommended strategic planning process
6	Board Profile	Description of required and desirable board member traits and expertise
7	The Board Chair	Summary of role and credentials of Chair
8	Frequency of Meetings	Suggestions for determining frequency of meetings each year
9	Good Board Meetings	Characteristics of good board meetings
10	Good Board Reports	Characteristics of good board reports
11	Transition Planning	Basic questions relating to CEO transition
12	Orientating New Board Members	Checklist of actions in orientation of new board members
13	Committee Effectiveness	Principles for board committee effectiveness
14	Annual Affirmation Statement	Sample statement for board members
15	Board Executive Session	Basic questions on executive sessions
16	Board Evaluation	Checklist of board's evaluation of itself, its individual members, and the CEO

Chapter 1

1. Jim Collins, "Good to Great and the Social Sectors" (monograph published by Collins), © 2005, Jim Collins, Author's Note.
2. Outi Flynn, "Hedgehogs and Flywheels," *Board Member*, March/April 2006.
3. Collins, "Good to Great and the Social Sectors," p. 3.
4. Even though this practice has been criticized in light of the recent corporate scandals.
5. Pat Bradshaw (ed.), "Nonprofit Governance Models: Problems and Prospects" (Ontario, Canada: York University, 2003), p. 11.
6. BoardSource, *Twelve Principles of Governance That Power Exceptional Boards* (Washington, DC: BoardSource, 2005); web site = www.board source.org.
7. Barbara Lawrence and Outi Flynn, *The Nonprofit Policy Sampler* (Washington, DC: BoardSource, 2006), p. xi.
8. Ibid.

Chapter 2

1. For more information on Carver's work, visit his web site at http://www.carvergovernance.com/ or policygovernance.com.
2. John Carver, *Boards That Make a Difference* (San Francisco: Jossey-Bass, 1997), pp. 134–135.

Chapter 3

1. For example, by Bob's estimate, in the last hundred board workshops that he has conducted, always including a presentation on a BPM, almost all the boards have supported the BPM concept. But perhaps twenty of them have debated whether they really need one, who should write it, and so on, and never actually got to it. Another fifty-five or so have assigned one or more persons to draft something and eventually do get it done, but that can be three or four years later! The remainder, perhaps 20 percent, have moved ahead smartly and adopted their own BPM within twelve to eighteen months.
2. If you do not have a committee with the responsibility for board training and development, you may want to discuss the BPM with another influential board member. The extent of your early conversations on the BPM will depend on the size of the board, how much counsel you need from the board leadership, and how much resistance you anticipate.
3. The Carvers' books include *Boards That Make a Difference, Reinventing*

Your Board, and *The Board Member's Playbook.* The full range of Board-Source books and pamphlets can be accessed on its web site, but the Governance Series provides excellent references for nonprofit board members. Booklet 3 in the Governance Series (Charles Dambach, p. 27) includes a case for a policy manual that is similar to our discussion in Chapter 2.

4. Among the materials listed in Appendix B is a sample presentation that you may find useful in preparing your presentation.

Chapter 4

1. Jim Collins, *Good to Great and the Social Sectors* (monograph published by Collins), © 2005, Jim Collins, pp. 23–27.
2. Miriam Carver and Bill Charney, *The Board Member's Playbook* (San Francisco: Jossey-Bass, 2004), p. xi.

Chapter 7

1. John Carver, *Reinventing Your Board* (San Francisco: Jossey-Bass, 1997), p. 18.
2. We use the word *section* to refer to each of the numbered items within a part. Some call them paragraphs and subparagraphs. What is important is that you adopt a set of terminology and that all board members and staff use it when referring to the BPM.

Chapter 8

1. John Carver, *Reinventing Your Board* (San Francisco: Jossey-Bass, 1997), p. 94.
2. Ibid.
3. Jim Collins, *Good to Great*, p. 42.
4. Ibid.
5. See Chapter 11 on the Board Reference Book.
6. To preserve the independence of the audit and compliance committee.
7. The Sarbanes-Oxley Act of 2002 defines a "financial expert" in general terms as someone who:
   • Understands financial statements and generally accepted accounting principles and is able to assess their application.
   • Has experience "preparing, auditing, analyzing or evaluating financial statements" that are comparable in scope and complexity to those of the company.
   • Is familiar with internal controls and financial reporting procedures.
   • Understands audit committee functions.
8. For example, BoardSource has a series of six booklets called its "Committee Series," which includes booklets on board structure, the executive committee, the finance committee, the development committee, the governance committee, and advisory councils (Washington, DC: BoardSource, 2004).

Chapter 10

1. *Nonprofit Governance Models, Problems and Prospects*, (York University, 2001); paper originally prepared for ARNOVA Conference, Seattle, Washington, 1998, p. 13.

Chapter 11

1. Miriam Carver and Bill Charney, *The Board Member's Playbook* (San Francisco: Jossey-Bass, 2004).
2. Although this *Playbook* assumes that the reader has developed a policy manual written in the format prescribed in the Policy Governance model, the principles for using the policy manual for solving problems and making board decisions are the same for organizations with their policies assembled in the BPM format.
3. Ibid., p. xi.
4. Ibid., p. xii.

Chapter 12

1. From Miriam's Kitchen's web site: www.miriamskitchen.org.
2. From TGen's web site: www.tgen.org/about/index.cfm?pageid = 1.
3. From AOG's web site: www.aogusma.org/aog/aboutaog.htm.
4. From World Vision's web site: www.worldvision.org/worldvision/master.nsf/ home_gc2_2006.
5. From Miriam's Kitchen's web site, www.miriamskitchen.org.

Afterword

1. BoardSource, *Twelve Principles of Governance That Power Exceptional Boards* (Washington, DC: BoardSource, 2005); web site = www.board source.org.
2. From Governance Matters web site: http://governance1.web132.discountasp .net/web/NGIG/print.aspx.

Index

207

Made in the USA
Lexington, KY
20 August 2017